The Clay Marble

and Related Readings

McDougal Littell
A HOUGHTON MIFFLIN COMPANY

Evanston, Illinois   Boston   Dallas

Acknowledgments

Farrar, Straus & Giroux, Inc.: *The Clay Marble* by Minfong Ho. Copyright © 1991 by Minfong Ho. All rights reserved. Reprinted by arrangement with Farrar, Straus & Giroux, Inc.

McFarland & Company, Inc., Publishers: "All the People of Khmer Were Very Troubled" by Ven Yem, from *Indochina's Refugees: Oral Histories from Laos, Cambodia and Vietnam*, edited by Joanna C. Scott. Copyright © 1989 by Joanna C. Scott. By permission of McFarland & Company, Inc., Publishers, Jefferson, NC 28640.

Alfred A. Knopf, Inc.: "Oppression," from *Collected Poems* by Langston Hughes. Copyright © 1994 by the Estate of Langston Hughes. Reprinted by permission of Alfred A. Knopf, Inc.

Curtis Brown, Ltd.: "Birthday Box" by Jane Yolen. Copyright © 1995 by Jane Yolen. First appeared in *Birthday Surprises: Ten Great Stories to Unwrap*. Published by Morrow Junior Books. Reprinted by permission of Curtis Brown, Ltd.

Continued on page 181.

The editors have made every effort to trace the ownership of all copyrighted selections found in this book and to make full acknowledgment for their use. Omissions brought to our attention will be corrected in a subsequent edition.

Cover illustration by Theresa Smith.
Author photo: Courtesy Minfong Ho.

ISBN-13: 978-0-395-77155-6   ISBN-10: 0-395-77155-2

Printed in the United States

17 18 2266 13

4500419043

Contents

Contents

The Clay Marble

Minfong Ho

For the little girl
who gave me a clay marble
on my first day at the Border

Preface

Cambodia's long and rich history dates back over one thousand years, to when the magnificent Buddhist temple complex of Angkor was built. For centuries, Cambodia remained a powerful kingdom, periodically expanding and shrinking in border wars with neighboring Thailand, Laos, and Vietnam. In the last two centuries, it survived French colonialism and World Wars I and II relatively unscathed, and then managed to remain neutral throughout most of the Vietnam War.

During the 1970s, however, the United States, the Soviet Union, and China backed various political groups in Cambodia, and Cambodia became more and more polarized, until open conflict broke out.

In 1975, the same year the Communists "liberated" Vietnam, the Communist Khmer Rouge declared victory in Cambodia. What happened under that regime during the next four years was a nightmare for the Cambodian people. They were shut off from the rest of the world, and more than one million men, women, and children were killed. It wasn't until Vietnamese troops invaded Cambodia, and Cambodians had a chance to flee their country, that the outside world began to realize the awful suffering inflicted upon the Cambodians.

Night after night, scenes of gaunt, wide-eyed Cambodian refugees were broadcast on television news programs. Unable just to sit and watch, I took a leave of absence from Cornell University in the spring of 1980, and returned to Thailand, where I had grown up. There I joined an international relief agency and helped to set up supplementary feeding programs for children living in refugee camps along the Thai-Cambodian border.

I remember my first day at the Border. There are no words to describe the intensity of suffering I saw there. The sickness, the starvation, the sheer silence of this vast sea of people overwhelmed me. I wanted to shut my eyes, turn around, and go back home.

Then I felt a small hand on my arm. Looking up at me was a ragged little girl. She held one palm out to offer me a small round ball of mud. I took it, then impulsively bent down and scooped up some mud from a nearby puddle, and rolled my own clay marble. When she saw that I was offering her this marble in exchange for the one she had given me, her face broke out into a beautiful wide smile.

Within minutes, children were crowding around to show me their homemade toys—clay marbles and buffaloes, rag dolls, fish made from strips of banana leaves, trucks created out of tin cans. The intricacy of the toys was wonderful, but it was nothing compared to the radiance of those children's laughter.

I saw these refugees then for what they really were: not the victims of war but its victors. They were the people who had, against all odds, survived, determined to start their lives over again.

I don't know what happened to the little girl who gave me that clay marble. Maybe she went home to Cambodia with a fresh supply of rice and rice seed and tools, to try to make a new life for herself and her family. Or maybe she stayed on at the Border, one of a quarter-million other refugees still living in camps there.

Whatever she did, life could not have been easy for her. Today, Cambodia is still at war with itself, despite many attempts to come to a peaceful settlement.

The other evening, as I was strolling along the Mekong River just eighty miles upstream from Cambodia, I saw a group of children playing on the riverbank. They were rolling marbles out of the damp clay, and I stopped and asked for one. Smiling, they put a clay marble, still cool and damp, in my outstretched hand.

I have it on my desk. And although I have long since lost the other marble, I can hold this one, and look at the green rice plants swaying outside my open window here, and hope with all my heart that the little girl who gave me that first clay marble is safe and happy, home in Cambodia.

Minfong Ho
Vientiane, Laos, 1991

Chapter 1

I heard a cowbell. At first it was such a faint tinkling sound that I thought it was just the wind in the trees, or the shrill cry of cicadas. I looked around. Dappled shadows stirred under a thick canopy of wild tamarind and rain trees, but there was no sign of life on the narrow trail stretching out ahead of us. I held my breath, and kept listening.

Yes, there it was again: the clear, quiet tone of a bronze bell.

"Sarun, listen!" I cried. "Can you hear it?"

My older brother turned to look at me. "Hear what?" he asked.

"A cowbell."

Sarun straightened up beside me in the oxcart and reined in the pair of oxen. Without the crunch of their hooves on the dry leaves, the forest seemed eerily quiet.

"I don't hear a thing," he said.

"I don't either, Dara," my mother added. She was sitting in the back of the cart behind us, on a thin layer of straw.

"Well, I heard it," I said. "A bronze cowbell. A big one—probably shiny, too." I could imagine it gleaming in the afternoon sunlight as it swung from the neck of a strong young bull.

"Which direction was it coming from?" Sarun asked. "Can you tell?"

I pointed to the reddish glow of afternoon sunlight filtering through the trees.

"Due west," my brother said thoughtfully, starting the oxen on their way again. "That's where we're headed. Maybe we're getting close to the Border."

"That's what you've been saying for days," I snapped, my hunger making me irritable.

Sarun glanced over at me and tried to smile. "Maybe we'll actually reach it tonight. Then we'll have grilled fish and fresh white rice for dinner. How does that sound?"

"I want something now," I said.

"But you just had breakfast," my mother broke in gently. There was a bit of straw in her hair, and she looked tired and discouraged.

"That was just a handful of cold rice," I protested. "Besides . . ."

Sarun gave me a warning look. Quiet, it said, don't make Mother any unhappier.

I remained silent. The only sounds were the rustling of leaves above and the creaking of cartwheels beneath us.

Then my stomach growled. "We would have been better off if we had stayed at home," I mumbled.

Sarun heard me and looked annoyed. "Stayed home? For what?" he asked. "There's nothing there. No food, no seeds, no animals."

I thought of our village. Sarun was right, I admitted silently. It was just an expanse of dried-up rice fields now, with a crumbling temple and flimsy huts. In the latest spate of fighting, the Khmer Rouge soldiers had even set fire to our houses and rice barns, so that the invading Vietnamese soldiers wouldn't be able to claim them. But that had left us with nothing to eat, no rice seed with which to plant our next crop of rice, not even a house to live in.

It had not always been like that, though.

I remembered happier times, when I was just two or three years old, and the smiling round-faced Prince Sihanouk ruled Cambodia. Our little village was a peaceful and prosperous place then, the rice fields green and calm, the harvests plentiful. At weddings and on temple feast days, I had sat curled in my mother's warm lap, nibbling at some sticky rice and coconut, sleepily watching the familiar faces of my father and brother, cousins, aunts, and grandparents dancing by the light of a kerosene lamp in the temple courtyard.

But then the fighting and bombing had started. At first the war had been distant and mysterious. Tiny silver airplanes, like fishes in the sky, would fly over us before disappearing into the horizon. Then the bombing had come closer, so close that the bombs shook the soil beneath my bare feet. My father and the other farmers in our village dug trenches where we all hid, crouching, at the sound of the approaching planes. For months, bombs were dropped around us, sometimes as often as five or six times a day, and many of the villagers were killed or hurt by shrapnel.

Gaunt young Communist soldiers dressed in black came down from the hills to tell us that it was the American imperialists who were bombing us. Kill the imperialists, they exhorted us, and kick out Prince Sihanouk. But that was like being told to catch evil spirits—so faceless and far away were the pilots in their airplanes and the Prince in his palace.

Yet, remote as they seemed, they must have been defeated, because the bombing stopped. Soon the Communist soldiers took over the village, announcing that they had "liberated" us.

Liberation turned out to be a long nightmare of hunger and misery. And fear—always that cold, silent fear.

My brother and most of the other young men in our village were sent miles away to dig ditches with huge work crews. Most of the women and children were allowed to remain at home, but we had to work much harder than before, and always under the watchful eyes of the armed soldiers. We never got enough to eat, and were sometimes fed only rice gruel and boiled banana stalks at dawn and dusk.

One night my father was roused from his sleep and taken away by two soldiers. We found his body the next day, at the edge of the forest. Had he been killed because he knew how to read and write and had taught the village children their alphabet? Or perhaps because he had gone to catch some snails in the fields for my grandmother to eat because she was sick and dying? I will never know. I knew only that I was not allowed to ask about him, or even cry when I missed him.

Over and over again we had been told by the Khmer Rouge soldiers that Cambodia was one big family, and that the Communist Party was our parent. And yet, in trying to create a new "family," the Communists destroyed my own family, ripping apart parent from child, brother from sister, husband from wife. It made no sense to me, since I could not understand how these shrill young soldiers could be my parents, but I did not dare ask.

Three years passed like one long nightmare, the kind where you are gripped by such a cold dread that you are unable to wake up from it.

Finally, shortly after I turned twelve, Vietnamese soldiers in green uniforms marched into our village, sending Pol Pot's Khmer Rouge soldiers on the run, and "liberated" us again. In the confusion, while the two armies were busy fighting each other, Sarun and some other farm boys escaped from their work crew and made their way home.

What a strange reunion that was—so muted and sad.

Father was dead, Mother told Sarun. And Grandmother as well. Describing how other relatives had died or disappeared, Mother started to weep, but Sarun stopped her. "It's not time to grieve yet," he said. "This is our chance to save what's left of our family. The Khmer Rouge butchers are in retreat, and the new Vietnamese-controlled regime doesn't seem to have much power over us yet. We've got to try and put our own lives in order now."

And he told us of his plans to cross overland through western Cambodia to the border between our country and Thailand. He had heard rumors of a refugee camp called Nong Chan, located on the Thai-Cambodian border, where free food and tools were being handed out. "Thousands of farmers all over Cambodia have made their way there," he told us. "That's our only hope, to go there and stock up on food and rice seed and other supplies. Then we can come home, repair the house, replant our fields, start our lives over again."

Mother shook her head wearily. "How can we know if the fighting will ever stop?" she asked. "Or if the Khmer Rouge won't win back control of the country? How will we know that we can ever live in peace?"

"We won't know, Mother," Sarun said gently. "But at least we can try."

Quietly my mother looked at the scorched earth around her and then, without another word, dug up her small silver amulet of the Lord Buddha from where she had buried it years ago beside the bamboo grove. Then we hitched up our oxcart and started the long journey westward.

That was nine days ago, and our meager supply of food and our strength were running low. Yet there was still no sign of this Border. Instead, we had caught so many glimpses of fighting and bloodshed on the main roads that we decided to take to the small dirt paths winding through the forests. Sometimes we met other people traveling in small silent groups, on foot or in oxcarts like ours. But beyond exchanging a cautious greeting or some brief directions, no one ever talked to us. Once we met some Vietnamese soldiers on patrol who saw us before we could hide, but they made no attempt to stop us.

By Sarun's calculations, we should have been at this refugee camp at the Border two days ago. I stole a glance at him now. What if he was wrong, and there was no such thing? The thick forest stretched out in front of us quiet and dark. There seemed to be no end to it.

Then I heard it again, the distinct sound of a clear bronze bell in the distance. It was coming closer. I sat up straight and noticed that Sarun had cocked his head toward the sound. So he had heard something, too.

Then I saw it.

Smooth and polished, the bronze bell flashed in the afternoon sun. It was dangling from the neck of a milk-white Brahman bull, who slowly emerged from the shadows of some teak trees.

"I told you!" I said triumphantly.

Sarun just stared, awestruck.

The bull was pulling a cart heaped high with gunnysacks of rice, with plowshares, with hoe heads, with rope and even fishnets. So heavily laden was the cart that it swayed from side to side as it moved, creaking noisily.

As we watched, the wheels of the oxcart slipped into a deep rut and lodged there. The driver stood up in the cart and flicked his whip at the ox, urging it to pull. Nostrils flared, the bull strained at its harness. But it was no use. The cart did not budge.

Sarun jumped down from our oxcart and ran over to the other wagon. Nodding briefly at the driver, he gripped one of the spokes in the stuck wheel and began to push. The other man climbed down and joined him. For some time there was only the sound of grunts as both men applied their weight on either side of the large wooden wheel. Then slowly, inch by inch, they eased it out of the rut, and the cartwheel rolled free.

The stranger wiped the sweat off his forehead with his sleeve. "Thanks, brother," he said.

"It's nothing," Sarun replied. "That's quite a load you have there."

The man laughed. "Everything a person could want," he said.

Sarun circled the cart. There was a small tear in one of the sacks, and he squeezed something out of the slit, onto his hand. I heard him gasp.

"What is it?" I asked.

Wordlessly he came over to me and stretched out his hand. Cupped in his palm were some grains of rice, each one still encased in a protective shell of thin, brown husk.

"Rice seed," he said, his voice soft with wonder.

My heart leaped: rice seed. Rice not just to eat but to grow. Looking at the brown husks cupped in my brother's hand, I felt that we could really go home and plant a good crop after all.

"Where did you get this?" Sarun was asking the other man. "Is there any more?"

"Any more? Brother, is there any more water in the sea? Is there any more soil on the ground?" The man laughed again, a deep, throaty laugh. "There's more rice there than I've ever seen in my life! Husked rice, long rice, short rice, sticky rice, fragrant rice . . ."

"And rice seed?" Sarun prompted.

"Rice seed? Listen, if they stacked up all the bags of rice seed there, they'd have a pile as high as the Cardamom Mountains!"

"And all this was at the Border?" Sarun asked.

"It's not just rice, brother," the other man went on. "Why, they've got enough tools there to build another Angkor Temple, and enough fishnets to catch all the fish in Tonle Sap lake!"

"Tell me where!" Sarun asked, his voice urgent. "Was it at the Border?"

"Of course," the stranger said. "At Nong Chan."

Sarun swallowed hard. "Nong Chan?" he repeated. I could see the lump in his throat bob up, then down. "It's true, then? Those rumors of free food and supplies at the refugee camp. It's all true?" It was not really a question but a plea.

I realized then that despite my brother's assurances to us, he must have had doubts all along.

The stranger sensed the tension in Sarun and grew serious. "If I laughed too much just now," he said, "it was not because I was joking. No, it's just that the happiness keeps jumping out of my throat. Yes, brother, it's all true, what they say about the Border."

"And there's more there? For free?"

"Just stand in line, and they practically throw things at you," the man said, and laughed again.

Behind me, I saw my mother bow her head over her silver amulet and pray. "Thanks be to the Lord Buddha," she whispered.

And although for the past three years I had not prayed, so that now I could barely remember the words with which to speak to the Buddha, I bent my head and gave thanks, too.

Chapter 2

The last rays of afternoon sun were filtering through the forest as we approached the Border. Gradually the trees thinned out and the path widened. Several trails merged into ours. It seemed as if all the paths out of Cambodia were converging on this one spot on the Thai border.

I could barely contain my excitement. I imagined mountains of rice lining the horizon, and piles of tools and fishnets everywhere. Perhaps there would even be mounds of sweet moist coconut cakes and banana fritters. "Hurry," I urged my brother.

Yet, as we finally emerged from the forest, all we could see was a vast barren plain dotted with shrubs and scraggly trees, flat and desolate. Overgrown clumps of fireweed and red sorrel stuck out from patches of buffalo clover, and then even those gave way to the cracked, hard soil of paddy fields in the dry season.

As we drove farther through the scrubland, though, I noticed that there were signs of life in the distance, of people and oxcarts so far away that at first they looked like black specks. Sarun urged our oxen on, and soon we could see more evidence of human activity. The branches of the few trees around had been chopped bare for firewood, mudholes had been dug for buffaloes to wallow in, and makeshift fences had been built around small vegetable gardens. We drove past these and approached the fringe of the refugee camp itself. It looked like an endless brown sea of thatched lean-tos, mingled with bright blue patches from clusters of plastic tents.

Spirals of smoke from countless cooking fires broke up the vast flatness of the landscape.

We passed women taking down laundry from lines, children spinning tops near the makeshift shelters, and quiet groups of people sitting around chatting. Why did it look so familiar and yet so unusual?

And it suddenly struck me: everyone was part of some family—not the cold-blooded Khmer Rouge version, the state as family, but a living, laughing, loving family.

I looked around in wonder. Even though many people seemed to be only fragments of a family—a frail grandmother with several young toddlers, or a group of young boys clustered around a few old men—they were a family just the same. Like a patchwork blanket, I thought, the people here were survivors of families who had been ripped apart and then joined again.

And everyone seemed to be busy doing something. Not just sitting alone silent and hollow-eyed with hunger, or organized into huge groups digging endless ditches. No, the people here were preoccupied with countless different chores of their own. I saw a sinewy old man splitting firewood; children lining up to draw buckets of water from a well; boys scrubbing their buffaloes in a shallow mudhole nearby; sisters combing each other's hair. And because it was getting close to dinnertime, there were women cooking everywhere. I could smell rice steaming, salted fish sizzling in hot oil spiced with chili, peanuts roasting—I even thought I caught a whiff of coconut cakes!

"It's like coming home," Mother said, with quiet wonder.

I knew exactly what she meant. Nong Chan was a

strange place unlike anything we had ever seen before, a vast barren field teeming with refugees. But in the bustling quiet of dusk, it had the feel of our village during the years of peace before the fighting had started, when farmers would come in from the fields as their wives fanned the charcoal fires and their children bathed with fresh well water.

Driving our oxcart, Sarun maneuvered the oxen through the scattered campsites until it became too crowded for the animals to move easily. He jumped down and led the oxen by the reins, threading his way carefully among the families. He headed for a well near a forked tree, where there was also a shallow creek in which buffaloes were wallowing. Several clusters of people were already settled there, with their thatched lean-tos and small fires, but nearby there was some empty space that no family had staked out for its own yet.

"This looks like a good spot," Sarun said, turning to Mother. "It's only going to get more crowded farther in."

Mother nodded, and together we got off the cart and started to unload our few belongings while Sarun unhitched the oxen.

"Poor things, you've both earned a rest," he murmured to them, patting the animals' thin flanks as he led them off to the water hole nearby.

Mother looked around for a place to set down her kettle and sleeping mat.

A girl spoke up. "Put your things over here, if you like." She was kneeling, stirring a pot of bubbling rice, and smiling up at us.

Mother set down the kettle she was holding, and I helped her put her sleeping mat beside it.

"Welcome to Nong Chan," the girl said. She looked about Sarun's age, eighteen or nineteen, and had a broad face with high cheekbones. There was a bright checkered kerchief wrapped around her hair, and her eyes were friendly and curious. "Where do you come from?" she asked.

"Siem Reap," Mother answered.

"Really?" The girl brightened. "So do we! Our village is right next to the lake."

"That makes us practically neighbors," Mother said, squatting down companionably beside the girl. "How many of you have come over to the Border?"

"There's four of us: my grandfather and my two little cousins," the girl said.

"And your parents?"

"Dead," the girl said simply. "As are my sisters, and the parents of the cousins with us." She gave the pot of rice a quick stir. "My grandmother and three brothers, too. All dead."

"My husband died four years ago, and then my mother," Mother said.

For a moment there was silence. I had heard enough of such conversations not to interrupt. First there were the greetings, then the terse tally of the dead, then the pause. Only after that, it seemed, could there be talk of other things.

The girl fanned the cooking fire before dipping a twig into it. "Let me help you get your fire started," she said. "It's getting late, and you must be very hungry." She extended the glowing twig to my mother.

Mother looked at the twig, but made no move to accept it. "There's really no need," she said awkwardly. "We really . . . I mean, we don't . . ." We don't have any more rice to cook, I knew she wanted to say, except that she couldn't bring herself to admit it.

"Of course!" the girl exclaimed. "You don't have

any firewood. How could you have gathered any? You just got here. Kindling is getting scarce, I can tell you. Most of the trees have been stripped bare—even the roots have been dug up for firewood. Here." She shoved a bundle of kindling toward Mother. "Use this for your fire."

Mother bit her lips. "No," she said, almost curtly. "You keep it."

The girl frowned, then her expression cleared. "Grandpa says my tongue's quicker than a raging river, but my mind is as thick as mud!" Using a tin cup, she scooped rice out of a gunnysack and stirred the grains into the pot already on the fire. "It's a good thing I just started cooking," she said cheerfully. "Won't have to start another pot. I'll just add some more water, and we'll have enough for all of us. There!" She looked up at me and my mother. "You will join us for dinner," she said. It wasn't a question, or even an invitation, but a simple statement.

"No, it's all right," my mother said stiffly. "We're not hungry."

The girl reached out and put her hand on Mother's arm. "You don't understand," she said gently. "It's different here. We have enough to eat. We have more than enough."

Then she must have seen the tears brimming over in Mother's eyes, because she turned away and started to stir the rice vigorously.

Before long the girl had Mother peeling a clove of garlic and crushing dried red peppers. I could tell that my mother was enjoying cooking again, now that there was seasoning and even some salted dried fish to work with.

Next the girl turned her attention to me. "I'm going to bathe while the rice is cooking," she said.

"Want to come along, little sister?"

I hesitated.

"Not shy, are you? My name's Nea. What's yours?"

"Dara."

"Well, come on, Dara. I've got a bucket of clean well water here we could share."

There was nothing I would have liked more than to douse myself with cool water just then, but I could see no hedge, no mud-brick wall, not even a line of laundry, to bathe behind.

Nea must have sensed my shyness, because she laughed as she tugged at me. "You've got to do everything out in the open here," she said cheerfully. "Come on, it's easy once you get used to it."

I followed Nea as she carried her pail of water to a massive beam of solid stone half-sunken in the fields. "My grandfather says that it might have been the crossbeam over the gateway of an ancient temple during the Angkor Empire," Nea said, pointing to the stone. "If so, it'd be almost a thousand years old."

I looked at the stone beam curiously. Chiseled on it were some whorled markings, worn smooth with time. On one corner of it was a carving of what must have been an *apsara*, a dancing angel. But all that remained now was a delicate hand, its stone fingers arching gracefully back as if in the middle of a dance. Gently I touched one fingertip, and felt as if I had reached across a thousand years.

"How did it get here?" I asked.

"Grandpa Kem isn't sure. Maybe it was the spoils of war, taken from some famous faraway temple like Angkor, or maybe there are some small ruins nearby that nobody even knows about."

Then, without even looking around, Nea hitched

her sarong up to her breasts and deftly stripped off her shirt. Scooping some water out of her bucket with a dipper, she splashed the water over her bare shoulders.

"Come on," she called, sprinkling some on me.

How wonderfully cool the drops of water felt. Clumsily I wrapped my sarong around my chest, too. Just as well I'm still flat-chested, I thought, as I wriggled out of my shirt.

Together, taking turns with the dipper, we bathed out in the open. I scooped ladle after ladle of water over myself, feeling the cold seeping through my scalp and down my shoulders. After those long, dusty days in the creaky oxcart, it felt so refreshing that I laughed out loud, and Nea laughed along with me.

When we had used up all the water, we walked back toward the carts, swinging the empty pail between us. As we approached the cooking fire, Mother looked up at us and smiled. I felt as if someone had suddenly reached inside me and squeezed my heart, so strong and happy was my mother's smile. I couldn't remember when I'd last seen her smile like that.

"Dinner's ready," Mother announced, pointing to a dish of salted fish stir-fried in garlic, and the pot of steaming rice. "Hope I didn't make it too spicy."

I started to head for the food, but felt Nea tugging at the pail.

"Come on," she was saying nervously. "Let's get into some dry clothes."

Only then did I notice that my brother was nearby, and staring open-mouthed at us. Not at me, I realized, just at Nea. I looked at my new friend. Beads of water glistened on her bare shoulders, and her wet sarong clung to her. I felt annoyed at my brother for staring like that, but one look at him, and I relented. All those years Sarun had spent digging ditches, I thought, he'd probably never seen a girl as lovely as Nea. Or as wet.

By the time I had changed into dry clothes, and joined my mother and brother by the cooking fire, an old man and two children were also sitting there. Mother edged closer to Sarun to make room for me, so that the three of us formed a semicircle around the flames.

Nea started ladling out the rice, and as she did so, she introduced the old man next to her, a tall gruff man with thick eyebrows. "This is Bou Kem, my grandfather," she said.

I nodded at him shyly.

"What do you say?" Mother prompted me.

"Grandpa Kem," I said obediently, and Mother nodded her approval.

On her other side, Nea explained, were her two cousins. One was a girl about my own age, and the other was a plump baby. I barely nodded to each of them before turning my attention to the rice.

Nea handed the first plateful to her grandfather, who took it without comment. She passed the next plate to my mother, who hesitated, then thanked her softly. Sarun was next. When Nea stretched out her hands to offer him a plate, he would not take it.

"Sarun, come on," I whispered.

He pretended not to hear me, and kept stoking the fire, sending a few sparks spinning up into the air. Torn between his hunger and his pride, Sarun couldn't seem to decide whether to accept or refuse Nea's offering.

"Please eat something, brother," Nea said softly, smiling at him across the fire. "It has been a long hard trip, and you need to keep your strength up."

He looked up at her, and finally he held out his hands and accepted the plate of rice from her.

My turn was next, and I almost snatched the plate from Nea. The fragrance of the long-grained rice was wonderful. Steamy and sweet and warm, it wafted up to me. I had not seen such a generous mound of white rice for a long, long time.

I lifted a spoonful of rice and ate it. I thought about what a wonderful thing it is to eat rice. First you let the smell drift up in lazy spirals, sweet and elusive; then you look at the color of it, softer and whiter than the surrounding steam. Carefully you put a spoonful of it in your mouth, and feel each grain separate on your tongue, firm and warm. Then you taste it—the rich yet delicate sweetness of it. How different it was from that gritty red rice we'd been rationed to, the last three years, gruel so bland and watery that it slipped right down your throat before you could even taste it. No, this was real rice, whole moist grains I could chew and savor.

I thought I was slowly relishing each mouthful, but before I knew it, my plate was empty. My mother had already started her second plateful, and Sarun was finishing off his third. None of my family had even bothered to try the fish in garlic sauce, we were enjoying the plain rice so much. I wondered if we were being too greedy. But Nea had noticed my empty plate and was already reaching over to ladle more rice on it.

"What about you?" Mother asked, glancing at the rest of Nea's family. "Will there be enough?"

"There's more than enough." Nea smiled. "That's what makes the rice taste so sweet here, don't you think?"

Nobody else said anything much, and soon we

were all done eating. Mother went off with Nea's young cousin to rinse off the plates at the well, while Sarun stayed by the fire to talk to Nea and her grandfather.

I strolled back to our oxcart and shook out my sleeping mat. Ever since we'd set out on this trip, I had slept under the broad wooden planks of the cart. In the unfamiliar darkness of the forest, it had been comforting to have those planks as a shelter. But I hesitated now, standing with my mat between the cartwheels.

Close by, the cooking fire was burning low, and a few sparks still whirled away into the night sky. Elsewhere, a boy was whittling a stick of firewood, and a baby was whimpering as its mother crooned to it.

On an impulse, I decided that I wanted to sleep under the open sky. So I spread my mat alongside the cart and stretched out on it.

The stars were just beginning to shine, and a cool evening breeze stirred the still air. In the distance, I heard a mother singing a lullaby. It had a familiar melody, one that I could remember my mother singing to me long ago. The pulsing hum of night sounds, of crickets and cicadas, settled over me like a light blanket.

As I shut my eyes, I took a deep breath. I had the strange feeling that somehow I had finally come back home.

Chapter 3

Sounds of splashing water and soft laughter drifted into my sleep. Drowsily I wondered who was taking a morning shower by the well in our bamboo grove at home. Then I blinked my eyes open, saw the silhouette of our oxcart wheel next to me, and remembered where I was.

The dawn sky was just beginning to glow, but already people were up and bustling about.

Nea was nearby, tending a cooking fire. Her face was as powdery-smooth as a lotus in bloom, and the morning light made her cheeks glow. Mother, too, looked refreshed and relaxed as she helped Nea fan the small fire.

I folded up my sleeping mat and stashed it in our oxcart. Quietly I walked over to them and sat down in my mother's lap. With her warmth behind me, and the flames in front of me, I felt very snug and secure.

"Really, Dara, you're too big to sit like this," Mother said, but she made no move to push me away. Instead, she started to stroke my hair.

Nea smiled at us. "Sleep well?" she asked.

I nodded, too content to say anything.

Mother held me for a while longer, then nudged me aside. "There must be something Dara could help with?" she asked Nea.

"Well, you could help carry some water back from the well," Nea suggested, smiling at me. "Jantu's there right now."

"Jantu?" I asked.

"My cousin. You met her last night, at dinner."

Vaguely I remembered the girl sitting across the

fire from me, but at the time I had been too engrossed in the steaming white rice to pay her any attention. I had no idea what Jantu looked like.

"Don't worry, she'll recognize you," Nea said, laughing, as if guessing my thoughts. She handed me a bucket and waved me off toward the well.

I strolled past clusters of people, all busy preparing for a new day. There was nothing to mark one campsite from another, but I could sense where one family's space ended and another's began. Like raindrops merging at the center of a lily pad, the members of each family gathered around their own cooking fire, a child often cradled in the lap of its mother's sarong. As far as I could see, the campsites stretched in every direction, their brown thatching relieved by flowered sarongs fluttering on laundry lines, or trays of red chili drying in the sun.

I soon reached the well. It had been dug in a small clearing and fenced in by a wall of scraggly branches. Pivoting on a tall post next to the well was a bamboo pole with a bucket dangling on the end. Dozens of children were lined up, waiting their turn to dip the bucket into the well. They all seemed to know one another, and there was a lot of jostling and teasing. I looked around for Jantu, but couldn't find her.

"Hey, over here!" I heard someone call. I turned and saw a tall, thin girl waving at me, with a chubby baby balanced on one hip. "You're Sarun's sister, right?" the girl asked.

I nodded.

"I'm Jantu," she said. Her shoulder-length hair was pulled back from her face and fastened with a shiny metal clasp. She brushed a strand of hair behind her ear impatiently as she looked at me. "How old are you?" she asked.

"Twelve," I said.

"Well, I'm thirteen," she announced smugly. Squinting against the light, she studied me for a moment. "Funny, you don't look much like your brother," she said. "He's good-looking, not like you." Behind her, some girls giggled.

I flushed. I had never thought of myself as pretty, but nobody had come this close to telling me I was actually ugly, either. I knew my sarong was muddy, and my hair uncombed, but another few buckets of well water would change all that.

I glared at Jantu and she watched me, grinning. I reached out and touched the baby's foot. "This your brother?" I asked her.

Jantu nodded, with a touch of pride.

"He's cute," I said. "Not like you."

The same girls who had just now giggled at me burst out laughing. For a moment Jantu looked taken aback, then she joined in the laughter, her eyes crinkling up.

I relaxed.

The baby started to squirm, and Jantu shifted him over to her other hip and jiggled him to keep him quiet. He had big round eyes and a thick thatch of shiny black hair. I reached out and tickled him. He squealed in delight.

"What's his name?" I asked.

"Nebut, but we just call him Baby. I take him to the lunch truck every day," Jantu said proudly. "That's why he's so chubby."

"What's the lunch truck?" I asked.

Jantu studied me a moment. "You could do with some visits to it yourself," she said. "That's where you get a free meal—a hot one. Any child who stands in line at one of the feeding stations gets a plate of food from the relief officials. You just bring your own plate and spoon. And the food's great!

Yesterday we had eggplant curry over rice." She rubbed her brother's round tummy and smiled. "Didn't we, Baby?"

I wasn't sure what Jantu was talking about, but before I could ask, it was our turn at the well. Jantu grabbed her bucket and walked to the pole by the well. As I hesitated, she turned around and flashed me a grin. "Come on, I'll show you what to do," she said. "Just follow me!"

After we had filled our buckets, I followed her back to our campsite. The four grownups were sitting around the fire, eating some of the leftover rice from dinner, and Jantu and I joined them.

After breakfast, Sarun started building a shelter nearby, hammering four bamboo poles into the ground and tying cross-poles over them. Mother draped some thatched roofing over the cross-poles, while Nea stitched together more roofing from palmetto leaves.

"Dara! Come help us," Mother called.

Soon I had strung up a laundry line between our cart and Nea's, and my spare sarong was flapping gaily in the breeze.

As a finishing touch, my brother hung a cloth hammock from the branches of a teak sapling nearby and invited Jantu and me to sit on it. As we sat there, swinging gently back and forth, I felt that I had settled down quite happily at the Border.

We were still swinging on the hammock early that afternoon when Jantu sat up and claimed that she could hear the faint rumble of the food truck.

"Come on!" she shouted, jumping off the hammock so abruptly that I nearly fell off. She rushed to her tent and grabbed a tin plate and spoon with one hand and her baby brother with the other.

"Hurry up!" she called. "And bring your own plate with you!"

With that she was off, running toward the sound of the truck, her brother bouncing up and down on her hip. I picked up my tin plate and spoon and followed her.

As we ran, we were joined by dozens of other children. They darted out of tents, from beneath oxcarts, and down trees, waving spoons and plates in the air as they headed toward the main road. From a tent nearby one little boy emerged clutching a bowl. His trousers slipped down from his waist as he started to run, almost tripping him. For a few steps he tried to hold on to his trousers as well as the bowl, then gave up and left his trousers on the ground in a heap, before continuing stark naked. I laughed, and kept running after Jantu.

I could see the food truck now. Churning up clouds of dust, it careened down the winding dirt road, stopping next to a signpost that had a big red "3" written on it.

"Quick, we have to get in line!" Jantu shouted.

By the time we got to the truck there was already a big crowd of children there. I held on to Jantu's shirt as we jostled for a place.

Under the noonday sun, the string of children wound far across the bare, dusty fields. There must be hundreds of us here, I thought. Most were about five or six years old, but there were some older children as well. Like Jantu, they often carried a baby on their hip.

At the front of the line, two huge pots had been unloaded off the truck, and a burly man was ladling out food from them. Two other men stood nearby, hoisting the empty pots back to the truck and carrying more full ones down the ramp. A young woman in khaki trousers and short hair looked on from the truck, earnestly writing in her red notebook.

When my turn finally came, I held out my plate just as all the other children in front of me had done. My mouth watering, I watched the man ladle out a mound of steaming white rice and splash another ladleful of some yellow squash stew over it. Just the smell of that stew, I thought happily, could fill me up and float me away!

Behind me, Jantu awaited her turn. Patiently she held out her plate for her share of food, as I stood off to one side.

Then, careful not to spill even a drop of the stew, we threaded our way over to a bit of shade under an acacia tree and sat down. Jantu was very good to her brother, spoon-feeding him the best parts of the stew, even though I knew she must be hungry, too. As for me, I dug right in, wolfing down huge mouthfuls.

All around me were children eating, their heads bent over their plates. "You know," I said between mouthfuls, "my brother kept saying there'd be food at the Border, but I didn't quite believe him."

"And now you do."

"That's the strange thing. It's still hard for me to believe it," I said. "It's almost too good to be true."

Jantu laughed. "This is nothing," she said. "Wait till you see what they give out at the real food distributions—for the grownups. That's even better!"

I sat back, leaning against the tree, and breathed a deep sigh of contentment. There was a morsel of meat left on my plate, which I had been saving till last. Slowly I spooned it up and swallowed it. How could anything be better than this?

Chapter 4

The very next evening, when my family and Jantu's were gathered around the cooking fire for our dinner, the topic of the food distribution came up. As the grownups talked about it, I held Jantu's baby brother in my lap and listened quietly.

Every two weeks or so, Nea said, a convoy of massive trucks arrived at Nong Chan, bringing basic food supplies such as rice, cooking oil, and salted fish. "Until you get your rations, my family can share ours with you," she said. "That's what happens all over the camp: the families who arrived earlier sharing with those who come after them. It all works out in the end."

"But how do we get our own rations?" Sarun asked.

"Well, a few days before the trucks are due, word generally spreads around the whole camp that there will be a distribution soon. Then, as head of your family, you'll have to join up with a team of other refugee families. Each team then gets registered with the relief officials," Nea said. "I think there's due to be another distribution in about five or six days. You should join up with a team now so you can register for that distribution."

It all sounded rather complicated to me. "Could . . . could we join your team?" I asked shyly.

Nea laughed. It was a soft, melodious sound, like the faint tinkling of temple bells in the breeze. "Why not?" she said. "It feels as if we're already part of the same family, doesn't it?"

I nodded happily. Yes, that was exactly how it felt. Just living next to each other these last couple of days, sharing meals and chores and stories, our families, I felt, had grown very close.

Impulsively I held the baby up and hugged him. He felt heavy and solid. He squirmed and wriggled loose. Only then did I notice the warm, dark stain on my sarong where he had wet it. Laughing, I handed him back to Jantu.

Just as Nea had said, we soon heard that a convoy of trucks was due to arrive at Nong Chan by the end of the week. Sarun joined Grandpa Kem's team and, along with the other men in their team, walked the two miles from the fringe of the refugee camp, where we were living, to the other edge, where the long thatched shelters of the camp headquarters had been built. There they registered their team with the relief officials, and were told to return in two days.

At dawn on the appointed day, when Sarun and Grandpa Kem hitched up one of the oxcarts, I begged to be allowed to go along, too. Much to my surprise, they agreed to take me.

Our team drove through the sprawling outskirts of Nong Chan on six oxcarts. I sat wedged between Sarun and Grandpa Kem on our cart. Craning my neck to see around, I began to understand how large the refugee camp was. I had heard the grownups estimate that there were at least forty thousand people here, but I had no sense of what that meant. Now I could see how the massive waves of refugees like ourselves had turned the flat, abandoned fields of Nong Chan into a teeming camp of thatched tents and plastic shelters that stretched out toward the horizon. If I were a tadpole weaving my way through a big, flooded seedbed, I thought, and each rice seedling were a refugee family, that might be about how big this camp is!

Finally we came to the heart of Nong Chan. Under tall bamboo watchtowers, we parked our oxcarts in a sandy lot packed with thousands of other people and their carts. All that morning we waited. It was hot and dry, and there wasn't a spot of shade anywhere, but nobody complained.

At about noon I saw a huge cloud of dust on the horizon. Soon a line of trucks roared down the dirt road that linked Nong Chan to the Thai town of Aranyaprathet, thirty miles away. The trucks ground to a halt in front of the entrance of the refugee camp, where the dirt road ended.

"Fifty-three trucks," Sarun said, his voice awed. "Now what?"

The tailgate of each truck swung down, and immediately groups of men with yellow armbands started unloading the sacks of rice, swinging and tossing the heavy gunnysacks from man to man with a swift, rhythmic motion.

As the rice was being unloaded and stacked into huge piles twice my height, officials with red armbands ushered the first registered team of men into corrals where sacks of rice had already been placed. Team by team, the men rushed in, hauled away the sacks allotted to them, and quickly left to make room for the next team.

I watched, awed by the almost clockwork precision of it all. There were thousands of men waiting before our turn came, but the distribution went so quickly and smoothly that we didn't have to wait long at all.

When it was our turn, and the bamboo gate of the corral was flung open to us, I climbed up and sat on the fence as the men on our team charged right through. I watched Grandpa Kem and Sarun carry a sack between them, staggering slightly under its weight. As soon as they reached the oxcart, they swung the sack up and over into the cart, then immediately went back for more. With the other men working as quickly and precisely, soon all our team's oxcarts were fully loaded.

Gasping for breath, Sarun wiped the sweat from his forehead with his checkered scarf as he eyed the filled oxcarts. "Now let's go show the women what we've got!" he said. As if he were heading a triumphal procession, he drove the team's first oxcart back through Nong Chan as the others rumbled behind.

As we approached our campsite, I saw Jantu jump up from the hammock and heard her shout, "They're back!"

In a flash, Nea and Mother and a dozen other women dashed out of their shelters, craning their necks toward us. Sarun sat up tall and straight next to Grandpa Kem and me. He was trying to look dignified, but when he saw Mother running up to greet him, he broke into a wide smile. "Look in the cart," he told her gleefully, reining the oxen to a stop.

Inside our cart were large, bulging gunnysacks, stacked neatly on top of one another.

"Rice!" Mother said softly.

"Yes, and something else, too," he said. His eyes searched the crowd until he found Nea. She was standing a little apart from the crowd, her face framed by a bright scarf. Looking straight at her, he pointed at the gunnysack next to him. "Something special," he said to Nea. "Look."

"Fragrant rice?" Nea asked, making her way toward our cart for a look.

"Even better than that," he said, waiting for her to come closer.

It was only when she got within a few steps of us

that she made out the words stenciled in green on the sack. "Rice seed," she read out loud, and looked up at Sarun with shining eyes.

"A special rice seed," Sarun said. "We were told by the officials that it has been treated against insects and mildew, so that almost each grain should germinate. And it's of a fragrant, high-yielding variety of rice, too."

Nea looked impressed. Stepping up to the cart, she touched the sack of rice seed and said, "You have so much of it. Three sacks?"

"Four," Sarun said proudly. "And we were also told that at the next distribution there would be hoe heads, and fishnets as well!" He jumped down from the cart and stood smiling beside her. "We can really plan ahead now, for the next planting season."

Nea looked up at him, then demurely lowered her eyes. Her voice was soft when she spoke. "You'll need help, planting all that rice seed," she said.

"I hope to find some help, sowing and transplanting it," Sarun answered. I had never heard his voice so gentle before. I jumped off the cart and edged toward them, not wanting to miss a word.

"Your mother and sister can help," Nea was saying.

"My mother is getting old, and my sister is still young," Sarun answered.

"You'll have friends from your village who'll be glad to help," Nea said. "Strong friends. Pretty ones, too."

"I think I have a friend right here," Sarun said, "who's stronger and much prettier than anyone back home."

Listening to them, I was reminded of the village folk dances at harvesttime, when the pairs of young men and women would dance the ramwong, slowly circling each other, their fingertips sometimes touching.

"It's a good village," Sarun was saying, his voice soft and warm. "At the edge of Tonle Sap lake, where the soil is black and moist. Our harvests are good, and there's plenty of fish fresh from the lake." He paused and smiled at Nea. "You'd like it there," he said.

Nea started to walk away. "How can you be so sure that I'd like it there?" she asked, looking over her shoulder at my brother.

"There's only one way to find out," Sarun said, walking after her. "Come with me, when we go home."

I started to follow them but suddenly felt a sharp tug at my arm. Jantu stood beside me, trying to pull me away. I resisted, but she was stronger, and managed to drag me with her.

"But I wanted to listen to them!" I said angrily when we were some distance from Sarun and Nea.

"I know!" Jantu snapped, still gripping my arm. "But anybody could tell they wanted to be alone. Your mother moved off, didn't she? So did Grandpa Kem."

I hadn't noticed, but now that Jantu mentioned it, I saw that my mother had quietly retreated to her own thatched lean-to, and Grandpa Kem was talking to the other men. I frowned. "But why?" I asked.

Jantu gave me an impatient look. "Why else do you think a man and a woman might want to talk alone?" she asked.

Sarun and Nea were strolling away from the oxcart, still deep in conversation. Nea's face glowed with a kind of bashful admiration, while Sarun gestured eagerly as he talked. They looked as if they were in a world of their own.

A startling new thought occurred to me. "You mean they're going to get married?" I blurted out.

Jantu grinned. "Who knows? The monsoons won't start for weeks yet and we have to go home to plant the rice crop," she said. "A lot could happen before then!"

I looked at the oxcart Sarun had driven back. The other team members were now dividing the sacks of rice and systematically carrying them off into the shelters of the various families. Soon we would be heading home with farm tools, new fishnets, and rice seed to start a new crop, a new life. I felt a quiver of anticipation and joy so strange to me that it was a while before I recognized it for what it was: a sense of hope.

Chapter 5

The days at the border passed quickly. I enjoyed spending my time with Jantu, since she was usually outgoing and friendly. Sometimes she would come up with new ideas about what to play, and sometimes she would just sit in the shade and tell me stories.

What I enjoyed listening to most were the folktales she told, some of which I had heard before from my own grandmother, but many of which were new to me. One of my favorites was about Khong the Brave, a coward who bragged that he had killed a tiger when it was actually his wife who had beaten it to death. "How can a woman kill a tiger?" he sneered. "I'm the one who did it!" When the King heard about it, Khong was commanded to lead the Cambodian army into battle on a huge elephant. In his terror, Khong accidentally jabbed the elephant's eye with his spear. Howling in rage and pain, the elephant charged into the enemy ranks, scattering them, and Khong the Brave became a true hero.

Jantu would pace back and forth excitedly as she told the story, her eyes sparkling as she acted out the part of the tiger, then Khong, then the elephant, all the while bouncing her baby brother on her hip. I would listen to her, spellbound, amid a small audience of other children.

Sometimes Jantu also used folktales to explain things to me. Not all children grow up with one war being fought after another, she said. In other places, and even in Cambodia during peacetime, children grew up without seeing a single soldier! Then why are there all these different armies fighting each other now, I asked. Even on the Border, there were separate military base camps made up of Khmer Rouge soldiers, Khmer Serei soldiers, and Khmer People's National Liberation soldiers, not to mention the Vietnamese soldiers to the east and the Thai soldiers to the west—all fighting one another. None of it made any sense to me.

"Don't you know the story about the family of deaf men?" Jantu answered, a mischievous gleam in her eye. Four deaf brothers, she said, were living together quite happily until a crocodile wandered into their house.

The oldest deaf brother shouted out a warning, pointing to the crocodile.

The second deaf brother, seeing his elder brother with the crocodile, thought they were going to attack him, and grabbed a stick to defend himself.

The third deaf brother thought the other two were planning to kill him, snatched up a knife, and brandished it around.

When the fourth deaf brother saw his brothers waving their weapons at the crocodile, he threw a rock at it. The rock bounced off the crocodile's hide and hit one of the brothers. Within seconds, all four deaf brothers were screaming and fighting each other as the crocodile slipped out the door.

"You see?" Jantu concluded with a shrug. "The leaders of Cambodia are just like those four deaf brothers, fighting among themselves because they cannot hear one another."

As much as I loved listening to the stories she told, what fascinated me even more were the things she made.

It amazed me, the way she shaped things out of nothing. A knobby branch, in her deft hands, would be whittled into a whirling top. She would weave strips of a banana leaf into plump goldfish or angular frogs. A torn plastic bag and a scrap from some newspaper would be cut and fashioned into a graceful kite with a long tail. A couple of old tin cans and a stick would be transformed into a toy truck.

Whenever Jantu started making something, she would withdraw into her own private world and ignore everything around her. Leaving me to mind her baby brother, she would hunch over her project, her fierce scowl keeping at bay anybody who might come too close or become too noisy. But if I was quiet and kept my distance, she didn't seem to mind my watching her.

And so I would stand a little to one side, holding the baby on my hip, as Jantu's quick fingers shaped, twisted, smoothed, rolled whatever material she happened to be working with into new toys.

"How do you do it?" I asked her one day, after she had casually woven me a delicate bracelet of wild vines.

"Well, you take five vines of about the same length—elephant creeper vines like this work well— and you start braiding them, see. Like this . . ."

"No, I don't mean just this bracelet," I said. "I mean the goldfish, too, and the kites and toy trucks and . . ."

"But they're all different," Jantu said. "You make them different ways."

"But how do you know what to make? Is there some . . . some kind of magic in your hands, maybe?"

Jantu looked puzzled. "I don't know," she said, turning her hands over and examining them with vague interest. They looked like ordinary hands, the fingernails grimy, the palms slightly callused. "I don't see anything there," she said. "Nothing that looks like magic." She shrugged and dismissed the subject.

Yet the more I watched her, the more convinced I became that Jantu's hands were gifted with some special powers, some magic. How else could anyone explain how she made that wonderful mobile, of two delicate dolls husking rice?

Even from the start, I knew it was going to be something special. For three days Jantu had kept me busy scrounging up a collection of old cloth and string. Then, as I sat cross-legged watching her, she fashioned two straw dolls in sarongs and straw hats and, with dabs of sticky rice, glued their feet onto a smooth branch. Carefully she tied strings connecting the dolls' wrists and waists, so that when one doll bent down, the other one straightened up. Each doll held a long thin club, with which, in turn, one would pound at a tiny mortar as the other doll lifted up its club in readiness. Jantu held up the mobile and showed me how a mere breath of wind would set the two dolls in motion.

Pound and lift, up and down, the two dolls took turns crushing the rice with exactly the same jerky rhythm that real village women pounded it to get the brown husks off. There were even some real grains in the miniature mortar set between the two dolls. It was the cleverest thing I had ever seen.

Children crowded around Jantu, pressing in from all sides to watch her work it. "Let me hold it," I begged, standing next to Jantu. "I helped you find the stuff for the dolls."

Jantu nodded. Breathlessly I held it carefully and blew on it. It worked! One of the dolls bent down and pounded the mortar with its club. The other doll straightened up and waited its turn. I was still engrossed with it when someone shouted a warning: "Watch out, Chnay's coming!"

Even in my short stay at the camp, I'd heard of

Chnay. He liked to break things, and he was a bully. An orphan, Chnay had made his way to the Border alone. Too young to be recruited into the resistance army, Chnay roamed the fields by himself, scrounging for food and sleeping wherever he liked.

Chnay sauntered up and shoved his way through to us. "What've you got there?" he demanded.

"Nothing," I said, trying to hide the toy behind me.

Laughing, Chnay snatched it away from me. One of the dolls was ripped loose and dropped to the ground.

As I bent over to retrieve it, Chnay pushed me aside. "Leave it," he said. "That's for kids. Look what I have." He thrust his arm out. It was crawling with big red ants, the fierce kind that really sting when they bite. "I'm letting them bite me. See?" he bragged. Already small fierce welts were swelling up on his arm, as some ants kept biting him.

"That's dumb!" I exclaimed. Dodging behind him, I tried to snatch the mobile back from him.

Chnay flung the toy to the ground, scattering straw and red ants into the air.

I grabbed on to his hand, but he was taller than I, and much stronger. He shoved me aside and stomped on the dolls until they were nothing but a pile of crushed sticks and rags. Then, kicking aside a boy who stood in his way, Chnay strode off, angrily brushing red ants off his arm.

I squatted down beside the bits of dolls and tried to fit them together, but it was no use. The delicate mobile was beyond repair. I could feel my eyes smarting with angry tears. "I should've held on to it more tightly," I said bitterly. "I shouldn't have let him grab it away from me."

Jantu knelt next to me and took the fragments of

the dolls out of my hands. "Never mind," she said quietly, putting them aside. "We can always start something new."

"But it took you so long to make it," I said.

Idly Jantu scooped up a lump of mud from a puddle by her feet and began to knead it in her hands. "Sure, but the fun is in the making," she said. She looked down at the lump of mud in her hands with sudden interest. "Have you ever noticed how nice the soil around here is?" she asked. "Almost like clay." She smoothed the ball with quick fingers, then rolled it between her palms.

When she opened her palm and held it out to me, there was a small brown ball of mud cupped in it. "For you," she announced.

I looked at it. Compared to the delicate rice-pounding mobile, this was not very interesting at all. "I don't want it," I said. "It's just a mud ball."

"No, it's not. It's a marble," Jantu said. Her eyes sparkling, she blew on it. "There! Now it's a magic marble."

I took it and held it. Round and cool, it had a nice solid feel to it. I glanced at Jantu. She was smiling. Slowly I smiled back at her.

Maybe, I thought, maybe she did put some magic in the marble. After all, why else would I feel better, just holding it?

Chapter 6

After that marble, Jantu was interested only in playing with clay. She would spend the long afternoons crouched by the mud puddle by the stone beam, scooping up handfuls of moist clay to shape little figures.

For some reason, the massive stone beam attracted Jantu. She loved playing there. "It's so old, so solid," she said. "I like being near it. It makes me feel like a cicada molting under some big rain tree."

At one end of the stone beam she had propped some fantail palm fronds, to make a thatched shelter so that we could play in the shade. When we crouched under it, it was like being in a leafy cave.

We spent most of our spare time in there. I would sit on the stone beam, bouncing her baby brother in my lap, as Jantu sculpted her dainty clay figures.

"I wish we could always be together like this," I said one afternoon. "Don't you wish things would just stay the same?"

Jantu glanced up from the clay buffalo she was shaping and smiled at me. "But how can we always stay the same, Dara?" she asked. "We're not made of stone. You wouldn't want to lie half-buried in the fields for hundreds of years, anyway, would you?"

"No, I meant . . . I just meant that nothing nice ever lasts." I struggled to find words for what I wanted to say. "What we're doing now, just playing here together—I wish we could hang on to it, that's all."

Jantu put down the half-formed clay buffalo. "I know what you mean," she said slowly. "You try to hang on to older people—parents, uncles, grandmothers—and they disappear. You make friends, and they go off in different directions, never to be seen again. Everything crumbles, so easily." Absentmindedly she picked up a dirt clod and crushed it in her fist, letting the crumbs of dirt dribble out. "We don't even have real families anymore," she said. "Just bits and pieces of one."

I stole a glance at my friend. I knew Jantu had lost both her parents and an older brother during the long war years, but she never talked about it.

"What do you mean?" I asked carefully.

"What I have, and what you have," she said, "are leftovers of families. Like fragments from a broken bowl that nobody wants. We're not a real family."

"What's a real family, then?"

"A real family," Jantu said, "grows. It gets bigger. People get added to it. Husbands, mothers-in-law, babies."

I thought about this. It was true. My own family had been getting smaller, shrinking rather than growing. Was it just the fragment of a family now? "I'd like to be part of a real family again," I said wistfully.

"You could be," Jantu said. "And so could I."

"How?"

"You'll see. Watch," Jantu said. She started molding her clay buffalo again. With small twisting movements, her hands teased out four legs, then shaped a pair of horns. Deftly she smoothed and rounded the shape until it had become a miniature water buffalo.

Then, with a flourish, she lifted up a layer of straw in a corner of our shelter. Nestled in the straw was a group of other clay figures. Carefully she set the miniature buffalo next to them. "There," she said.

"They're finished—the whole set of them."

"What are they?" I asked. "Can I see?"

Jantu smiled at me mysteriously. "I didn't want to show you until they were all ready."

"And are they ready?"

"They are!" Ceremoniously, Jantu took a clay doll and set it on the stone beam. Just then a few drops of rain started to fall.

Jantu parted a section of the palm frond and scanned the sky anxiously. Thick gray clouds had drifted across to block out the sun. In the distance, a clap of thunder sounded.

The wind picked up and was sweeping up eddies of dust into the air. Then the rain started in earnest, one of those sudden thunderstorms hinting of the monsoons due to come soon. Jantu stretched her sarong protectively over the pile of straw where her clay figures were. Hunched over them like that, she looked like a scruffy hen trying to hatch her precious eggs.

I huddled close to Jantu and listened to the rain drumming on the leaves. Raindrops pierced through the cracks of the palm fronds and felt light and cool on my bare arms. I thought of the long rainy afternoons I had spent on the porch at home when I was very young. As light and cool as the rain, my grandmother's fingers would massage my scalp while I rested my head in her lap. Nearby, the murmur of my family surrounded me, like a soft blanket.

I closed my eyes now and tried to imagine them all sitting around me: Grandmother stroking me, Father and Sarun whittling on the steps, Mother stoking the embers of the cooking fire. It wasn't just the thick thatched roof that had sheltered me, I realized now. It was the feeling I had had then, of being part of a family as a gently pulsing whole, so natural it was like the breathing of a sleeping baby.

When I opened my eyes, I saw that Jantu had a lost, faraway look in her eyes, and I knew that she was remembering, too, what it was like when her own family was whole and complete.

As the rain died down, Jantu turned to me and smiled. "You still want to play with my family of dolls?" she asked.

I'd rather have my own family back, I thought, but dolls were better than nothing. "Sure," I said.

"Wait, let's set things up for them first," Jantu said. She pointed to the puddle next to the stone beam. "That," she announced, "is the lake. The Tonle Sap lake."

It didn't look very impressive, but I knew Jantu well enough to realize that her tone of voice promised something more. So I waited.

"And this is our village, by the edge of the lake," Jantu said, sticking a tuft of weeds near the puddle.

She rummaged in the pile of straw by the stone beam and took out a small clay doll, about the size of her palm. "Now, this," she said, "is my cousin Nea." It was a lovely doll, with rice grains for eyes, and bits of black string for hair. It even had a scrap of red cloth draped around it for a sarong.

I looked more carefully at that doll. Not only was its sarong the same color as Nea's, but the way its one tiny clay arm rested on its hip, and the slight tilt of its head, reminded me of Nea.

"It looks like her," I said.

Jantu smiled, and set the dainty clay doll next to the tuft of weeds. "That's Nea at home," she explained. Then she took out two other dolls from the straw, one taller and the other smaller than the Nea doll. She held both out to me. "Who do you think these are?" she asked me.

Immediately I recognized Nea's grandfather, because that doll was holding on to a delicate wooden hoe. And the other doll was clearly Jantu herself, complete with a tiny clay baby hitched up on her hip.

"Grandpa Kem and you," I answered, with growing interest. "What about my family?"

"Right here!" With a flourish, Jantu pulled away the last layer of straw from the pile and revealed a miniature village, with a thatched farmhouse on stilts, oxcarts, a water buffalo, and three more clay figures. I saw that the two larger dolls were my mother and Sarun, and I had no trouble recognizing myself in the last doll.

"My hair isn't that messy," I complained.

Obligingly Jantu smoothed some of the black thread away from the doll's eyes and handed the doll over to me. "How's that?" she said. "And look, you even have a scarf, see? I saved you the best bit of cloth I had. Go on, you can wrap the scarf around her neck."

That's the nice thing about playing with Jantu, I thought happily, as I took the doll modeled on myself. She lets you join in the game. Carefully I wound the scarf around my doll, before setting it down next to the dolls of Mother and Sarun.

With that frown of concentration which meant she wanted absolute silence, Jantu arranged the dolls so that the two families were grouped on either side of the "Tonle Sap" puddle. The dolls stared at one another across the water.

"Now what?" I asked, impatient for the game to begin.

Jantu sat back on her heels and studied her arrangement. "Well, it's no use being friends, is it," she said, "when our families are going to go back to separate villages? I could shout myself hoarse by the side of Tonle Sap lake, and you'd never even hear me. But suppose"—and here she reached for the Nea doll with one hand and the Sarun doll with the other—"suppose this happened . . ." Jantu paused and bent over the two dolls. Her fingers were deft and light as she molded the clay. When she had finished, she held up the two dolls for me to see. Their hands were now linked by a dab of clay, so that it looked as if they were holding hands. "What do you think?"

"You mean, suppose Sarun and Nea got married?" I asked.

Jantu grinned. "Suppose they did?" she said. "Let's see what would happen."

Carefully she set the two dolls down in my village, next to the Mother doll. Then she pointed to the doll of herself, left on the other side of the lake. "What do you think would happen to me then?" she asked.

"You'd follow Nea, and come live with us," I said.

Jantu grinned. "Absolutely. Move me, go ahead, pick me up and move me."

Gently I picked up the clay figure of Jantu and her baby brother and moved them across the puddle to join "my" family. Left by himself, Grandpa Kem looked rather forlorn. "What about Grandpa Kem?" I asked.

"He goes, too. Move him, that's right."

I did, and saw that there was quite a clan on my side of the lake now, with Sarun and Nea, Grandpa Kem and Mother, Jantu and her baby brother and myself—all clustered around the thatched house. I liked that.

They looked like a real family.

"We'd need to build another house," I said, "for the newlyweds."

Jantu dipped her hands into the puddle and

scooped out a lump of clay. Deftly she shaped it into four walls and put some leaves on top of it for a roof. "There," she said. "What else?"

"How about some more animals?"

"I've already got plenty of those," Jantu said. She rummaged behind another part of the stone beam until she brought out a handful of little chickens and ducks and another water buffalo.

"And trees," I said. "We could plant some mango trees. My father loved mangoes."

Jantu hesitated. For a long moment she was silent. "My father liked mango trees, too," she said at last, and her voice was strange, as if a bit of rice had gotten stuck in her throat. "We had a mango orchard behind our house, at home," Jantu said. "Elephant-tusk mangoes. Sweet and long and smooth." She hugged her knees to her chest. "That's where they killed him, between the mango trees. I saw it. Father put his hands up to his face, just before they shot him, I think because he didn't want me to see him scared."

Had my father been scared, too, I suddenly wondered, when they took him away that night? But it had been dark, and I hadn't seen his face.

Jantu took a deep breath. "No mango trees," she said. "We'll plant lemons and guava and papaya trees instead."

I looked down at the puddle. Now it didn't seem like Tonle Sap lake, and the clay dolls looked sad and misshapen. "I don't want to play anymore," I said.

"Come on," Jantu said firmly. "How can you dream if you don't learn to shut off the thoughts you don't want?" She twisted a twig so cleverly that it really did look like a tiny lemon tree. "Here," she said. "That's where the orchard will be."

"All right," I said, and poked another branch

beside it. "And that can be the guava trees."

"We can even make some fruit to hang from the trees," Jantu said, and started to stick beads of clay onto the branches.

Then we made plows for the oxen to pull, and fishnets for the lake, and even a cradle for the baby twins that the Nea and Sarun dolls had.

We were just burying some real rice seeds in the furrows that the Sarun doll had plowed near the lake when I looked up and noticed that the sun was setting. The sky had cleared, and a beam of pale sunlight was shining on the miniature rice fields we had made. I knew that Mother would be calling us for dinner soon.

"Let's finish planting the field," I said.

Jantu nodded and poked a few more rice seeds into the moist soil.

By the time the field was planted, it was almost dark. The Nea doll was sitting near her cradle of babies, and Jantu gently rocked the cradle with one finger. "It's time to sing the children to sleep," she said.

And softly, in a sweet clear voice, Jantu sang a lullaby I had never heard before:

"When the rain is falling,
   When the rice is growing,
   When the day is done,
   Then my little one, my lovely one,
   Will come home to sleep—and dream."

As she sang, Jantu's eyes glowed with the twilight reflected in them. There was a long silence when her song ended.

"My mother used to sing that to me when I was little," she finally said.

"Teach it to me," I said.

And so, sitting on the ancient stone beam in the fading light, Jantu taught me the lullaby. I closed my eyes and rocked myself slightly as I sang, and thought of sleeping babies, and full harvests, and a home with a real family.

Chapter 7

The toy village became the center of our world, and Jantu and I played with it every day. Each time we would add a few more things—a rice barn, rain barrels, a pigsty—and as Jantu shaped them, we would make up more stories about our new lives after we left the Border.

Hard though we tried to immerse ourselves in this make-believe world, we could sense the growing tension in the real world around us. As we played with our clay dolls, I could not help but notice that more and more heavily armed soldiers were appearing in the camp, trying to recruit men. Sometimes they would stop at our campsite and talk to Sarun.

The fighting on the Border was growing more intense, they said. The Vietnamese soldiers inside Cambodia were mobilizing their forces for one last attack as part of their dry-season offensive, so the Khmer Serei resistance scattered along the Border had to recruit more men to counter the Vietnamese attack.

"But I don't want to fight," Sarun would say quietly. "I just want to stay through two or three more distributions to collect enough rice and other supplies. Then I'll take my family home before the monsoons, in time to plant the next rice crop."

What about his duty to his country, the soldiers would argue in soft, wheedling voices. Didn't he care about the sovereignty of his country? Didn't he want to help kick out the Vietnamese invaders, and at the same time keep the ruthless Khmer Rouge army at bay, so that there might be peace and prosperity in Cambodia again?

I listened to all this while playing with my clay dolls. How could people "fight for peace," I wondered. Why couldn't we just go home and grow our rice crops? I didn't care which side won, as long as we were allowed to go on with our lives in the village.

In our small make-believe world, at least, life was simple and easy to understand. There were no soldiers and no war, only people like ourselves quietly getting on with their lives. And so, as the soldiers tried to talk my brother into becoming a soldier, I made the clay Sarun doll plow his tiny rice fields.

Late one morning, shortly after Sarun had returned from the second mass distribution with hoe heads and fishnets, we heard the sounds of gunfire and bombing in the distance. At first I didn't even notice them, until Jantu suddenly lifted her head and listened.

Nearby, Grandpa Kem had stopped hammering on the stakes of the new lean-to he'd been building and was also listening.

"What is it?" Nea called to him from her thatched shelter.

"Hush!" her grandfather said.

I stayed very still and listened, too.

The sound was so faint that I thought it might be the lunch truck backfiring. But then the dull thuds grew louder and lasted longer.

"Bombs," Grandpa Kem said quietly. "They're shelling the Border."

It was the quiet, tired way he said it that scared me. As if he had known all along it would happen, and that he couldn't do anything about it. I looked at my mother, whose eyes were wide with fear.

"What do we do?" Mother asked Grandpa Kem.

"Start packing," he said. And without another word, he began putting his tools away.

So it was really happening. Even on the Border, the fighting was going to start again. I watched my mother fold up the sleeping mats and clothes into our oxcart, and Sarun load up some of the new hoe heads he had just been given. Mother was trying to pile in some kindling, as Nea and Grandpa Kem hurriedly loaded up their oxcart with their belongings.

I turned to our miniature village. Two dolls were plowing furrows in the fields, while another mended a fishnet. The latest addition, a baby doll in a hammock strung between the lemon trees, was peacefully asleep. I looked at them for a long moment.

"I'm not going," I said.

Jantu reached for a handful of straw and started to cover up the village. "Come on, Dara," she said. "It's just a toy. We have to go."

"I'm not going."

"We can come back to it later," Jantu said. She tugged at my sarong gently. "Come on."

Around us, people were already starting to move. My mother had her arms full of clothes and was yelling at me, "Leave those silly dolls, right now!"

Jantu and I exchanged a quick look. "We could take them," I said.

"They'd break," Jantu said.

"We can try," I said. "I'll carry them."

Jantu shook her head. "Things that can break," she said slowly, "are not worth taking." She picked up one of the clay dolls, and held it. "It's only what you can bring inside of you that really matters. How do you think I was able to say goodbye to my mother and father?" she asked, so softly that she seemed to be talking more to herself than to me. "When they died, I stored it up—everything I remembered about them, loved about them. That's what I bring with me. They're inside me now. Part of me. Do you know what I'm trying to say?"

I shook my head.

"Think about your own father, Dara. Tell me something about him. Something that makes you happy when you think about it."

As I tried to think, I heard the sound of shells exploding, like distant thunder. "I used to be scared of thunder," I told Jantu. "So Father would always hold me in his lap and cup my ears with his hands." And suddenly I could feel his hands tight against my ears again, strong and warm, shutting out all the noise, so that I was in our own snug, safe world. I looked at Jantu. "I understand now," I said. Gently I took the doll from her and left it on a bed of straw by the stone beam.

Within minutes we were on the move. Mother and Sarun had stashed whatever they could in the cart. With thousands of other refugees, we headed into Thailand, away from the shelling.

I had never seen so many people on the move before. Many of the other refugees had set out on foot, taking nothing but bundles of clothing with them. A few had their belongings strapped onto rusty bicycles, which they wheeled clumsily along. Others had baskets dangling from bamboo shoulder poles, filled with utensils and clothing and even children too young to walk.

Swept up by this current, Grandpa Kem drove his oxcart in front, while my mother, with Nea and

Sarun, followed in the cart behind him. Jantu, Baby, and I lagged farther behind the carts. They had offered to take Baby, but Jantu had wanted to hold him.

It was eerie, like a dream. Everyone was quiet. Instead of the usual noises of people arguing and laughing and talking, it was now utterly silent. Occasionally the dull boom of shelling would echo from the distance, but that, and the constant scuffling of feet over the dusty road, was all I could hear.

Somewhere along the way I lost my sandals. My feet were sore and hot, and I was very thirsty. I wanted to sit down in the shade and rest, but everyone else was moving, and so I plodded along, too, putting one tired foot in front of the other.

Once I heard a child crying, her shrill sobs cutting through the silence. Then I saw her—a thin little girl in a tattered dress, clutching a plastic doll by its leg. The doll had only two sockets where the arms should have been, and its long, yellow hair swept a semicircle in the dirt as it was swung to and fro. The girl was wailing for her mother, her voice broken and hoarse. Nobody paid any attention to her.

I stared at her until Jantu pulled me away. "Keep walking, or you'll end up like her—lost!" she said.

"But nobody's helping her. How's she going to find her mother?"

"She isn't," Jantu said.

"What's going to happen to her, then?"

"She'll probably get picked up by some soldiers and locked up in the orphanage they have for refugee kids, where they are forced to become slaves, or something."

"Really?"

"If you don't believe me, just start howling for

your mother, and see where you'll get locked up! Now come on!"

Shaken, I stumbled after Jantu, clutching on to her shirt so that I wouldn't lose her in the crowd. Ahead of us I caught a glimpse of my own mother, and felt reassured.

We passed several other children like the little girl with the doll, all of them howling for their parents, all of them bypassed by the hurrying grownups.

Everywhere, too, there were signs of the temporary homes that people had tried to build for themselves at Nong Chan—a hammock strung between two saplings, a neat ring of stones around a cooking fire, salted fish hung out to dry in the sun, a shelter woven from plastic bags and cardboard, now abandoned and looking forlorn.

I thought of the spot we had claimed for ourselves around our oxcart. I had liked the way that our damp sarongs fluttered on the laundry line, and that the embers of the cooking fire flickered within its neat circle of stones at night. I liked propping up our dishes to dry on the wooden rack Sarun had made, and our palmetto-thatched hut, which had become a snug, familiar home for me to curl up in at night.

Now it was gone. I thought of the small world of our clay dolls, and sighed. How senseless it was, to have cared about something so unreal.

We trudged on in the glimmering heat of a blazing afternoon sun. Once in a while I saw jeeps drive past at the edge of the crowd, with Thai soldiers in their olive-green uniforms pointing their guns into the crowd. At first I thought they were trying to stop the stream of people from moving farther into Thai territory, but then I noticed that jeeps were driving slowly behind us as well, as if to shepherd us along. When I asked Jantu about it, she just shrugged.

"They want to keep an eye on us. Make sure we're not wandering off into their fields." Across the stubbled fields was a cluster of thatched houses, set amid banana trees and bamboo groves. I even caught a glimpse of a little boy driving a flock of geese home.

So that was what it meant to be a refugee. We were farmers who had been displaced from our old land and yet prevented from settling on any new land. Would we always be on the move, people who not only didn't have a home but weren't allowed to build a new home anywhere?

By midafternoon I was very hungry. I had asked Mother to pack some cold rice in a basket, but there hadn't been any left over from breakfast, and so we had left our campsite without food. Jantu must be hungry, too, I thought.

What would the food truck have served today, I wondered. Stew with chunks of yellow squash and strips of pork? Or cabbage and kale seasoned with fish sauce? Certainly there'd be steaming hot white rice—and plenty of it! My mouth watered.

Just then, as if I had dreamed it into taking shape, I saw the food truck in front of me, parked in the shade of a long, thatched building.

I blinked. It looked abandoned, and therefore strangely neglected, but it was unmistakably the food truck.

"Look!" I said, tugging at Jantu's arm.

Jantu glanced at the truck, but kept walking.

"Wait! Can't you see the pots loaded on the truck?"

"Sure," Jantu said. "So what?"

"The pots could be filled with rice. And stew. Yellow squash stew!"

"We can't stop," Jantu said, but she looked more interested.

"We could take a look. A quick look. There's bound to be some food there. You could feed Baby. Come on, it won't take long."

Jantu hesitated. "All right," she said. "You catch up with your mother and tell her what we're doing."

So I ran ahead, ducking between the baskets and bicycle wheels until I caught up with Mother.

"We'll wait for you," she agreed reluctantly. "But don't take too long."

"I promise!" I called over my shoulder, and ran back to Jantu.

We climbed over the bamboo fence separating the road from the compound where the food truck was parked, and ran in.

In the middle of the compound was a large bamboo shed with a thatched roof. I dashed in. It was an enormous kitchen. There were about fifty huge charcoal stoves lining the side walls of woven bamboo strips, and another thirty even bigger stoves in the middle. Some of the stoves still had nuggets of glowing charcoal in them. The cooks had obviously left in a hurry.

The food truck was backed up right against a ramp next to the front door of the kitchen. It looked as if the pots had just been loaded onto the truck when the shelling began.

Jantu climbed up to the truck itself, and I handed Baby up to her. She lifted the lid of the first pot in the truck and peered inside. I waited breathlessly.

"Nothing!" she cried.

I followed her up the truck and peered inside the second pot. Nothing there either, except a thin layer of burnt rice. I realized with sharp disappointment that the truck must have been unloading dirty pots when the shelling started.

"So much for your yellow squash stew!" Jantu

said impatiently. "Now we'll have to run back to catch up with the others!"

Holding her brother firmly against her, she jumped off the tailgate of the truck.

Just then everything exploded.

The blast threw me off balance. I crashed into an empty pot, sending it spinning through the air. A shell had landed nearby, ripping apart the thatching of the kitchen roof and setting it on fire. Pieces of thatching collapsed onto the matted bamboo sides of the kitchen underneath. Within seconds the whole shed was in flames.

There were screams everywhere.

Outside the compound, people started to stampede. The stream of refugees had turned into a churning, swirling torrent. Like a river bursting its banks, people fled in every direction, scattering and running into the adjoining fields. The jeeps wove through the confusion, honking uselessly, trying to stem the flow.

I groped my way past the rolling pots and jumped off the truck. My one thought was to find Mother.

Then I saw Jantu.

My friend's arms were streaked with blood. She was sobbing, but she seemed unhurt. She was holding on to her baby brother, rocking him jerkily to and fro. I realized that the blood was spurting from the baby, from his plump little foot, which was twisted at a funny angle.

"He's hurt, help me, he's hurt!" Jantu said, sobbing. Baby was crying, too, howling so hard that his face was turning a purplish blue.

"I'll get help," I said. "Wait for me here." And with the sound of their wails ringing in my ears, I rushed off.

Chapter 8

I climbed back over the bamboo fence. The crowd outside had churned up so much dust that I could barely see to the other side of the road. How would I ever find my family among them? I fought off a wave of panic. Taking a deep breath to calm myself, I plunged into the crowd.

Almost at once I was knocked off my feet by the shoving and pushing. I got up and stumbled on. It seemed crucial to move along, if only to keep from being knocked down.

Before I had taken very many steps, someone jostled me. I grabbed blindly for support and fell, pulling down a boy next to me and tripping the frail old woman behind him as well. Dazed, they both sprawled next to me.

Quickly I got up and tried to help the old woman to her feet. But she only groaned and lay there. Already people were stepping on her sarong, her hair, her hands. Again I tried to pull her into a sitting position, but I couldn't budge her.

Desperately I grabbed at someone's sleeve and begged for help. But I was only brushed aside. The boy beside me was crying.

Finally somebody stopped and looked at us. To my great relief, he took charge.

"I'm bringing your grandmother over to that big tree. She'll be safe there," he said. "You follow me, all right?"

I nodded, and the man bent down and lifted the old woman up. As he carried her away, he shouted back at me, "Bring your brother! You want him trampled to death?" I grabbed the wailing child by the hand and stumbled after them.

There was a big tamarind tree by the side of the road, and when we got to it, I saw that there were at least six other people lying in its shade. Most of them had been wounded by the explosion, and blood still glistened on their skin. But one looked dead, a pale young woman whose eyes were locked in an unseeing gaze at the leaves above.

A man with a red cross on an armband moved among the wounded, rinsing off a cut, murmuring reassuring words. Amazing, I thought, I've managed to come to the right place for help.

The man carrying the frail old woman gently lowered her onto the ground, in the shade. I noticed that he also had on an armband with a red cross. He patted me gruffly and said, "She'll be okay. Just stay with her, and keep an eye on your brother."

"He's not my brother!" I protested. "But Jantu's brother, he's just a baby, he's hurt, back by the food truck. Please come!"

"All right, let's go," he said. Holding my hand, he led me out of the shade of the tamarind tree and back into the crowd.

It was like wading upstream against a strong current, to push against all the people rushing past the other way. I clung to the stranger's hand, and together we plowed our way back to the compound where the food truck was.

There Jantu was huddled against the wheel of the truck, holding her brother. For an awful moment I thought he was dead. But then the baby whimpered softly, and Jantu saw us.

"Over here," she called.

Without a word the man walked over and scooped the baby up in his arms. Then, turning briefly to make sure we were following him, he headed back toward the spreading tamarind tree.

He laid Baby down in the shade, next to the old grandmother. Jantu sat down cross-legged and cradled her brother's head in the lap of her sarong. "Thanks, Dara," she said faintly. "Thanks so much."

"You should thank him," I said, looking up at the stranger who had helped us.

He was examining Baby, rinsing off the blood from his hurt foot. It did not look nearly as bad when it was clean. There was a wide gash where the shard had sliced off some skin, but the cut itself didn't seem to go very deep.

"Will he be all right?" Jantu asked.

"His ankle might be fractured, but don't worry," the man said. "The ambulance should be along soon. They'll have medicine and bandages to treat the wound properly."

Soon a white truck with a big red cross painted on its side arrived, and parked next to the tamarind tree. Four men jumped out and quickly started examining each patient. One of them, a white foreigner with a bushy red beard, came to Jantu's baby brother and murmured something to the baby which we couldn't understand, but which sounded soothing. He examined the ankle, then called a Cambodian nurse over. They talked briefly before the nurse turned to Jantu.

"He says the child has to be hospitalized," the nurse translated. "They'll take him to the hospital inside the Khao I Dang refugee camp, where they can set the bone and watch him for a few days. It's not far from here."

"A few days?" Jantu echoed in dismay. "But he can't be alone that long! He's only a little—"

"Of course you'd have to go along with him,

child." She glanced at us. "Unless you have a parent or older relative to accompany him?"

Jantu hesitated. "I . . . I don't. I mean, I do, but I've got to find them first. You see, just now when the bombing . . ."

But even as Jantu was talking, the red-bearded doctor had picked up her brother and was carrying him into the white van. Jantu ran up to him, pulling at his sleeve to protest. He ignored her. Quickly he laid the baby down on a mattress on the floor of the van and gestured for Jantu to climb in next to the baby.

She turned to me in desperation. "What are we going to do?" she asked. She looked scared and confused.

"I don't know," I said. I felt every bit as scared as Jantu looked. "I guess you'll just have to go along with Baby."

"What about you?" Jantu asked.

"I . . . I'll come with you."

Jantu shook her head. "No, Dara, you've got to stay," she said. "You've got to find our families and tell them Baby's hurt, and in the hospital with me."

"They know where the hospital is," I argued. "Let them find us there."

"They won't look there, Dara. Don't you see, they'll just think we're lost."

There, it was out.

Lost: that single, terrifying word. I felt as if a rock had slammed against my stomach and lodged there. I had been thinking of it all this time, but was afraid to bring it up. Now Jantu had said it. We were lost. Just like that little girl with the broken doll, crying in the crowd. For a second I felt like wailing for Mother, too.

"You have to find them," Jantu said grimly.

I stared at her. "How?" I demanded.

"They'll be around." Jantu would not look at me. "Someone will be there."

"Where?"

"Nearby. Somewhere."

"But where? Where? Tell me where?" My voice shook.

"By the stone beam," Jantu said firmly, with some of her old authority. "They're bound to go back to our old campsite to wait for us. So just find your way back to our campsite, Dara. You can do it."

I shook my head. "No," I said. "I can't."

"You have to, Dara. It's the only way to link up with them again. And you know where our stone beam is. By the well, Dara."

"Which well? There're hundreds of wells like ours. How can I find the right one?" I was beginning to sound shrill, but I couldn't help it.

"You'll find it, Dara. And when you do, your mother and Sarun and Nea and Grandpa Kem—they will all be there, waiting."

"How do you know that?" I asked. "Suppose I can't find the stone beam? Suppose there's nobody waiting there for me?" I swallowed hard, trying to fight a mounting panic.

"You've got to try, Dara."

I took a look around. People were swirling past, like waves in a churning human sea. Thousands of faces, and not one that looked familiar.

With a stab of longing I suddenly thought of home—not of our makeshift shelter somewhere at the Border, but of my real home. I thought of Grandmother's little herb garden of basil and turmeric and lemon grass, soaking up the morning sunshine under her kitchen window.

"Oh, Jantu," I said, "I'm scared."

For a moment Jantu did not speak. Picking up a lump of mud, she kneaded it in one hand. "Of course you're scared," she said slowly. "It's a scary world out there. But we're here, and we're stuck with it, aren't we?" She started to roll the lump of clay in her hands. Her voice was as calm and rhythmic as the movement of her fingers, kneading the clay, shaping it. "We've got to do the best we can, out of what we've got," she said.

I watched Jantu's long fingers, her hands lightly cupping the clay, circling each other in a kind of fluid dance. And as I watched, the clay took shape, becoming rounder and smoother, smoother and glossier.

"Remember that marble I made after Chnay smashed my rice-husking dolls? I told you it was a magic marble."

I nodded, remembering how just holding that smooth, round marble had made me feel better.

"Did you believe me? Did you think it was a magic marble?" Jantu asked.

Again I nodded.

Jantu smiled. She continued to roll the ball of clay in her hands, sculpting it, rounding it. "I'm making you another marble, Dara," she said. "Except this one will be more powerful. It will have stronger magic in it." Her fingers stopped moving, and she opened her hand. Cupped in one palm was a perfectly round, perfectly smooth clay marble.

I reached out and took the marble from Jantu's hand. It was still moist and felt solid and heavy. Just moments before, it had been a lump of mud in a dirty puddle. Now Jantu had shaped it into a perfect sphere.

"Is it really a magic marble?" I asked.

Solemnly Jantu nodded. "It will make you strong,

and brave, and patient," she said.

"But will it help me find my mother?"

Jantu took a deep breath. "If you believe in it, it will help you," she said. She reached out and closed my fingers over the marble. "Now go," she said.

The sun was already low on the horizon, and a light breeze had sprung up. The shelling had stopped, and in the quiet I could hear skylarks singing in the fields. I took a last look at Jantu and the baby.

Then I turned away and started walking east, away from the safety of Thailand. My shadow stretched out long and thin in front of me. It would be dark before too long, I thought, but I would not be afraid. The magic marble was firm and smooth in my hand.

Chapter 9

I kept walking even after the sun had set. The sky was still tinged with gold, but I knew that soon everything would be swallowed up in darkness and I would have to stop searching for my family.

I had managed to retrace part of the way we had come earlier that afternoon, but I was nowhere near where our campsite had been. In the fading light I could make out the silhouettes of all the tall watchtowers in the distance, rising on their bamboo stilts above the desolate plains. I kept heading toward them, since they marked where the Nong Chan camp officially began.

It was already dark when I reached the watchtowers. Scattered campfires had been lit near them, as if other people found it reassuring to be sheltering near these landmarks. Families gathered quietly around the fires, sorting out their belongings, or bedding down for the night. Many others had not even bothered to build a fire, but were just huddled on the ground, sleeping under the open sky.

For a while I wandered from fire to fire, searching the faces of the people reflected in the firelight for someone I knew. But there was not a familiar face among them.

I noticed an old man looking at me curiously. He was sitting with his own family, holding a plate of cold rice. I looked at it hungrily, but could not bring myself to ask for any food. The old man smiled at me kindly.

Ask him, I told myself. If not for food, at least for some directions. I took a step toward him, then hesitated. What would I ask?

I wondered what Mother was doing now. Of course, she would be worried about me, I thought, but at least she would be with Sarun and Nea and Grandpa Kem. I imagined her stoking the embers of a cooking fire, at that very moment thinking of me. And perhaps Grandpa Kem, Sarun, and Nea would be sitting nearby, staring silently into the flames. Just imagining them all made me feel lonely. On the twilight horizon, a crescent moon was rising. I watched it hook on to a branch right above me, and dangle there, like a new sickle blade gleaming in the darkening sky.

If only I could climb up this tree to the moon, I thought drowsily, and curl up against its smooth curve, how comfortable I'd be tonight. Or I could hang on to it as it swept across the night sky, and search down far below for my mother.

Tomorrow, I promised myself, I will go on looking. Tomorrow I will find them. For now, the tree in front of me looked old and solid. I leaned against it, pressing my cheek against its rough bark. It seemed as good a place as any to rest. So I lay down under it and felt for Jantu's marble in my shirt pocket. It was there, smooth and round, reassuring. I took it out and, with it in my hand, fell asleep.

It was dawn when I woke up. A cool morning breeze was blowing, and I shivered, rubbing the goose bumps from my bare arms. Then I got up and stretched.

I was cold and hungry, but I felt a certain pride that I had survived the night alone, with only the clay marble for company. Maybe Jantu's magic is working, I thought. Maybe the magic in the marble is making me stronger and more sure of myself. Quickly I checked my pocket to make sure I had put it back, and then, taking a deep breath, I started to walk on again.

Already there were people up and about, many of them packing their bundles of clothes, ready to move on. I picked my way through them. I felt as if I were just about invisible, for all the attention anyone was paying me. I heard a group of men talking about the shelling yesterday, and I lingered there, eavesdropping on their conversation.

What I heard was disturbing. The shelling was expected to start again, someone said, except that today it might be coming from the other direction: from the west and aimed at the east. Would that be Thailand shooting back at the Vietnamese, or perhaps the various anti-Vietnamese Khmer factions shooting at each other?

The men discussed this at length, but nobody seemed to have any clearer sense of what to do than I did. What everyone did seem convinced about was that the fields here at Nong Chan would be unsafe for at least the next few days—maybe longer—and that we should seek shelter elsewhere. But where? Some talked about walking back into Thailand, perhaps toward the protected, more established refugee camps, like Khao I Dang. Others talked of joining one of the military base camps scattered deep in the forests beyond Nong Chan.

Listening to all this, I felt a stab of fear. If I didn't find the stone beam, it would be even harder to meet up with my family, as the continued shelling would scatter us yet farther apart. I had to find them, and soon.

But how?

I noticed that the kind old man who had smiled at me the night before was among the group of men I had just been listening to. Sitting a little off to the side, he was eating some cold rice out of a small woven basket. Slowly I approached him. He looked up at me and beckoned for me to come over.

"Where's your family, child?" he asked.

"I . . . I don't know," I said.

He shook his head sadly. "Got separated from them during the shelling yesterday, did you? I thought so. Look, I don't have much rice left. Take this." He held out the last bit of rice in his basket to me and said, "If you're hungry, why don't you try waiting for the lunch truck?"

Of course, the lunch truck! Why hadn't I thought of that before? The lunch truck was one of the very few things around that had its own set routine and destinations. People—especially children—would know where it stopped. I could ask for directions to the signpost with the red "3" painted on it. From there I could easily find my way back to the stone beam!

"Thank you," I said to the old man, taking the handful of sticky rice. And as I turned away, I also silently thanked the magic marble, for showing me the way.

People were still in a state of flux, looking for their old campsites or for someplace safer. I asked the first child I saw for directions to the lunch truck stop, and got them. I started walking, continuing to ask children along the way for further directions. By early afternoon I had managed to find my way to the truck stop where Jantu and I had so often lined up for our lunch.

The wooden signpost with the red "3" was still standing, although there wasn't a single child waiting at it.

I barely paused there. Everything was starting to look familiar. Almost running, I headed past the well.

Forgotten were my hunger and my sore feet. I wanted only to get home and throw myself into Mother's waiting arms. Should I slow down, and creep up to surprise Mother and Sarun? Or should I just keep running, and shout to get their attention? I could hardly keep from laughing out loud as I ran the last stretch home.

Suddenly I stopped.

There was nothing there.

The flat landscape stretched out, bleak and familiar. But there was no oxcart parked there, no laundry flapping nearby, no hammock strung under it. There was no campfire, no tarpaulin sheet draped over bags of rice and tools.

And there was no one from my family.

They must be nearby, I thought. Desperately I tried to find Mother or Sarun in the scattered crowd of people.

A mistake, I thought. I must have made a mistake again. I was at the wrong spot after all. I would just have to keep looking further. I glanced around, trying to get my bearings.

It was then that I saw our old stone beam half jutting out of the mud and, to one side of it, our toy village.

Or what was left of it.

The puddle that Jantu and I had pretended was Tonle Sap lake was still there, but the houses were gone, trampled into the mud. I walked over to the puddle and knelt down. From the mud I pulled up a twig that I recognized as our lemon tree. The tiny clay beads that we had hung on it had dissolved, and the twig itself was broken. I tried to stick it back into the mud, but it wouldn't stand.

Fragments of the dolls, now only bits of hardened clay, were scattered nearby. I crouched over the broken clay dolls and tried to piece a few of them together, but I couldn't even tell which pieces were part of which dolls anymore. There was a scrap of cloth that had been the Nea doll's sarong, and a pair of tiny clasped hands that had linked the Sarun doll to the Nea doll, but nothing else was even recognizable.

I laid my cheek down on the sun-warmed stone and pressed against the carved pattern on it. The carving on this one stone has survived a thousand years, I told myself. What does it matter that your silly clay dolls didn't make it through the night? I closed my eyes, but the tears trickled out just the same, until my cheeks were cool and slippery against the stone.

Chapter 10

"What are you crying about? Those stupid clay toys?"

Wiping my cheeks hastily, I looked up. It was Chnay, the bully who had once smashed Jantu's delicate mobile.

I swallowed hard and tossed the clay fragments into the puddle. For a moment, ripples webbed the surface, then disappeared. I stood up and faced Chnay. "You broke our clay dolls," I said.

"Not this time." Chnay grinned. "I know who did, though."

I looked at the flattened village and tried to shrug. "I don't care," I said.

"It was your brother," Chnay said.

"Sarun did that?" I did not believe it.

Chnay pointed at the ruts running through the toy village. "You see those cartwheel tracks? They're his."

"You saw Sarun drive off?" I asked. "And my mother?"

"What's the matter? Did you really expect them to sit around here waiting for you to show up?" Chnay laughed.

I knew he was mocking me, but I swallowed my pride and asked again if he had really seen them go off.

"Sure," Chnay said.

"When?"

"When what?"

"When did they drive off?"

"Well, it wasn't as simple as that," Chnay said

slowly, as if he was savoring my impatience. "They were here early this morning, all waiting around. They seemed to be very worried. Your mother was crying, and I heard her say she wanted to go look for you, but the others restrained her." He looked at me curiously. "What happened to you, anyway? Got separated and lost?"

I nodded impatiently, and told him how Jantu's baby brother had gotten hurt. "Then what?" I asked. "How come they aren't here now?"

"I'm coming to that," Chnay said slowly, clearly enjoying his power. "Well, this band of soldiers came by, armed with AK-47s and grenade launchers."

"What about the soldiers?"

"They started telling your brother how dangerous it'd be staying out in the open, and how he should move his family and supplies to their base camp, where the military would protect them."

"And so they left?" I asked. "All of them?"

"Well, your mother wanted to stay and wait for you, but Sarun insisted that she leave. Said the family shouldn't be split up any further."

I felt a sick, sinking feeling in my stomach. Abandoned: I bit down on my lips, very hard, to stop the tears from welling up. It had been so hard just to find the stone beam. How could I ever hope to find my family now that they had left the only landmark I knew? I looked around, past the people milling in the surrounding field, to the forest beyond. It seemed hopeless.

"Your mother was crying very hard," Chnay added helpfully.

"She'll be back," I said with a confidence I did not feel. "I'll just wait here for her."

"Didn't you just hear me? They decided it's too dangerous to stay out here in the open. Even if you stay here, they aren't going to come back for you. At least not for a while. You'd be better off going after them."

Reluctantly I considered this. I didn't like the idea of going off on my own again, but it did sound like a sensible thing to do.

"Where did they go?" I asked Chnay.

He pointed to the southeast. "See that rutted trail which leads out from the fields into the forest beyond it? They took that trail. Took all their precious rice supplies, both oxcarts, everything."

"Where does that trail lead?" I asked. "Aren't there several base camps out there? Which one did they go to?"

Chnay shrugged. "How would I know?" he said.

"Didn't they tell you?"

"Tell me?" Chnay laughed. "Who'd tell me anything? Nobody even sees me."

I looked at him. His hair was matted and unkempt, and all the buttons but one on his shirt were missing. For the first time I felt sorry for him, now that I had a taste of what it was like to be totally ignored, to feel unwanted. I could imagine him standing on the side, watching silently as my family bustled about, fretting, discussing, making decisions.

"So you really have no idea where they are?" I asked.

"I didn't say that. What I said was that nobody ever tells me anything. That doesn't mean I don't find out things for myself." He smiled smugly at me. There was a military base camp east of Nong Chan, he told me, where a large group of Khmer Serei soldiers lived. "Their leader is a man called General Kung Silor," Chnay said. "And he's actively recruiting men to join his army, to prepare a counterattack against the Vietnamese. If men join up now, he'll take them in, feed them and clothe them, and provide some shelter for their families." After the shelling yesterday, Chnay said, a lot of people apparently felt Nong Chan wasn't safe enough anymore, so hundreds of them had decided to join up with Kung's army and move their families over to the security of the base camp there.

"And that's where my family and Jantu's are now? At this base camp?"

"That's where I think they are," Chnay hedged.

"But you're not sure?"

He tilted his chin up belligerently. "Who can be sure of anything?" he said.

I felt very tired. My knees gave way, and I sat down heavily on the ground. I had no idea what to do next.

Chnay glanced at me, then rummaged in his pockets. He brought out a handful of cold rice wrapped in a strip of banana leaf. "Here, take it," he said, squatting beside me.

I looked at it hungrily.

"I can always get more," Chnay said, his hand outstretched.

I took it. I crammed a chunk of rice into my mouth and chewed. There was even some fish sauce flavor on it. I smiled, and Chnay smiled back at me. Why, he doesn't look mean at all when he smiles, I thought.

When I had finished his rice, I felt quite a bit better. "How far away is this base camp?" I asked.

"About three miles," Chnay said. "Through the forest." He squinted at the sun, then pointed slightly away from it.

"How long would it take to get there?"

"You should reach it long before nightfall."

"And the trails through the forest, are they well marked?"

"Should be. Besides, there'll be a lot of people heading that way. Just find someone who's going to join Kung Silor's army, and follow him."

"You make it sound so easy."

He shrugged. "Nothing to it."

I got up and dusted off my sarong. "Well, I guess I'll start off," I said. I took a few steps, then paused. "Thanks for the rice," I added.

"It's all right," he said. He was still squatting on the ground, hugging his knees to his chest. He looked small and forlorn.

I waved at him, and walked a few more steps.

There were people everywhere, but not a single one looked familiar, or paid any attention to me. I felt very alone. If I disappeared into thin air right now, I thought, nobody would even realize it. Except maybe Chnay.

I turned and looked back at him.

"Hey!" I called.

He was looking at me sideways, with one cheek resting on his drawn-up knees. "What do you want now?" he asked.

I took a deep breath. "Do you want to come along?"

For a moment he frowned, as if he didn't know what to make of this. Then his face brightened.

"Sure, why not?" he said, and grinned.

He got up, and together we started walking toward the forest.

Chapter 11

The path wound through the edge of the Nong Chan plain, and into the forest behind it. Everyone seemed to know where Kung Silor's camp was, so asking for directions was no problem, especially when we met up with some newly recruited soldiers who were on the way to the base camp themselves.

Still, it was a long walk. My bare feet, which had been sore from all the walking the day before, were tougher now. Perhaps they would soon be like Chnay's, I thought, so thick and callused that they wouldn't feel anything. For now, though, I still missed my sandals.

Just as I was about to suggest a rest, I noticed that the thickets of trees and bamboo groves had thinned out, and in the distance there was a clearing.

We could hear the sound of men singing, and cautiously we made our way closer. From behind some thick bushes we watched as rows of men, all carrying rifles, marched across the square of tamped-down earth. Following the loud commands of an officer, they paced up and down, sharply turning left or right at his every order. Then they lined up in the center of the square and faced the flagpole there. Starkly silhouetted against the twilight sky was the blue-and-white Khmer Serei flag. At a signal, they all saluted the flag, and started singing a strident song with words like "liberation" and "freedom" mixed with "blood" and "death."

"That's the national anthem for the Khmer Serei," Chnay whispered in my ear.

"Well, I don't like it," I whispered back. Perhaps it

was the lengthening shadows, or the presence of all those soldiers bristling with weapons, but I felt uneasy and scared.

Chnay led the way down a path that veered off from the square farther into the camp. We paused at a narrow wooden bridge that spanned a deep trench stretching along one side of the square. There were bamboo spikes on the bottom of the trench. I shivered.

"What do we do now? Do we start looking for my family?" I asked.

Chnay seemed uncertain and subdued. "I'm not sure," he said.

I looked around at the gathering dusk with deep misgivings. What were we doing in the middle of the dark forest, I wondered, with nowhere to go and nothing to eat?

As if sensing my thoughts, Chnay pointed to an abandoned lean-to with torn thatching for a roof, and suggested that we sleep there. Without waiting for my answer, he crawled into the shelter and curled up in the corner. As I hesitated outside, he beckoned me in impatiently. "Get some sleep," he said. "We'll look for your family tomorrow."

We? So Chnay was going to help me look for my family? I realized then that I had made a friend, and quietly crept under the thatching and lay down next to Chnay.

I spent a restless night, tossing about listening to the torn thatching flapping in the wind. The forest sounded strange and scary, alive with the grunts and shuffling of mysterious animals. I scrunched up into a small ball and waited for the morning.

At some point I must have dozed off, because when I opened my eyes, Chnay was standing over me, grinning. "Breakfast," he announced and, squatting next to me, held out some cold rice on a banana leaf.

"Where did you get it?" I asked.

"I took it," he said.

"What do you mean? Who did you take it from?"

Chnay looked annoyed. "Do you want it or not? If you're going to be so picky about where your food comes from, I can eat it up by myself."

"You stole it," I said.

With a defiant tilt of his chin, Chnay started eating the rice. "Not really," he said. "It's a kind of secret sharing, that's all. I just don't bother to tell the people that they're sharing their things with me. Anyway, food's meant to be eaten by the hungry."

I was about to protest when my stomach rumbled. Chnay was right, I thought. Food was meant to be shared. I reached out and broke off a chunk of the rice for myself.

That day, Chnay and I wandered around at the base camp, looking for my family. It was hard to know where to begin. If Chnay had not been with me, I would probably have been too timid and scared to do much more than huddle in a corner somewhere by myself. With his guidance, though, we began by slowly circling the outer edges of the sprawling base camp, where hundreds of new families had come for shelter.

It took the better part of the day just to circle the camp once, and by nightfall I was tired and very hungry. That night we returned to the spot where we had slept before and went to sleep with empty stomachs. I missed my mother terribly. It seemed so lonely to come back someplace and not have anybody to even ask you where you had been. Slipping my hand into my pocket, I rubbed the magic marble Jantu had given me. I knew that Chnay would only laugh if he knew about it, but as I drifted off to sleep, I held the marble in my hand and silently asked it to help me find my mother.

The next day we continued our search, making a smaller circle inside the first one, but again there was no sign of my family. The disheartening thing about looking was knowing that more families were coming in every day, as the shelling and fighting outside the camp had picked up again. And I couldn't go back to the stone beam to check if anyone was waiting for me there, since it was now too dangerous to walk back to the open fields at Nong Chan.

The only thing I could do was to wander around the military base camp, peering into the faces of every person I saw. I was surprised how I could slip in among groups of people and look at them without their taking the slightest notice of me. But as I began to know my way around the base camp, I began to enjoy being unnoticed. It meant I could be wherever I wanted, whenever I wanted.

I was also learning how to scrounge for food on my own. Unlike Chnay, I never actually stole food, but I found that if I edged up close to a family at their mealtime and stared, refusing to budge even if they tried to wave me off, they might offer me a scrap of food just to make me go away. Still, the handouts were never very substantial, and, more often than not, I would go to sleep hungry.

Late afternoon of the fourth day, Chnay and I had completed our sixth and smallest circle around the camp and had still found no sign of my family. The only area we hadn't yet covered was the military headquarters next to the big square where we had seen the soldiers saluting their flag that first evening.

"What do we do now?" I asked Chnay.

Chnay surveyed the area around us. Clustered around the square were a dozen thatched huts, the biggest of which was, Chnay told me, where General Kung Silor himself lived. Behind them were tents for higher-ranking officers, and nearby were the long thatched barracks for the enlisted soldiers.

"We could look around the barracks," Chnay said without enthusiasm.

"What's the use?" I said, on the verge of tears. "They won't be there." I was tired and discouraged and hungry, and everything seemed bleak. How could I ever hope to find my family when I didn't have the energy to go on looking for them?

It was then that I smelled it—something so wonderful that I was suddenly alert. Roast chicken: my nose was never wrong. My brother had often teased me about it, saying that I could sniff out ripening tamarind pods or guava fruit before even the bees got to them. I sniffed the air now and knew that it was roasting chicken.

The smell was coming from the cluster of thatched huts across the ditch, where the kitchen for the officers must be. I nudged Chnay. "Let's go take a look, over there," I said.

Quickly we made our way across the square to the cluster of huts. The smell of the chicken was stronger, and I was sure it came from a long thatched building near a large tent.

As we passed this tent, I saw a group of men sitting inside, on a platform built of split bamboo, their rifles leaning against them. At their center was a bare-chested man who seemed to be doing most of the talking, his voice a low, deep murmur. Gleaming against his brown chest was a large white crescent dangling from a gold chain that glinted in the late afternoon sun. As I stared at it, the man glanced up and saw me. He frowned, as if about to say something, but Chnay tugged at me, and I walked past.

We approached the kitchen and peered into the doorway. It was dim inside, and except for the flickering light cast by the charcoal fires, the long room was in shadow. Moving among the shadows were some people fanning the charcoal fires. And roasting over the glowing embers were rows of skewered chicken, the skin a glistening golden brown.

My mouth watered. I could almost taste the tender meat as I imagined biting into a piece, tearing at the crispy skin.

I glanced at Chnay. Without a word, the two of us crept closer. There was no one outside, and the doorway was unguarded, except for a little furry monkey chained to the doorpost.

Motioning for me to stay by the doorway, Chnay tried to slip in. The monkey bared its fangs at him and shuffled forward, dragging its chain noisily behind it. Chnay eyed it warily.

I saw a bunch of bananas hanging on the other side of the door, out of the monkey's reach. Quickly I twisted one off and tossed it at the monkey. It hesitated, then snatched at the banana, and Chnay was able to slip past. Keeping as close to the wall as he could, Chnay inched his way toward the closest row of chickens.

As I watched, my heart pounding, he darted out of the shadows and tore a drumstick off a roasting chicken. He looked around, saw that no one had noticed him, and quickly tore off another one. Then, flashing me a triumphant grin, he sprinted to the door.

I had been so engrossed in watching him that I

hadn't seen the monkey finish its banana and dart back to the doorway. When Chnay ran out the door, it suddenly lunged out, screeching.

Startled, Chnay kicked at it, but missed. Yammering furiously, the monkey hurled itself at Chnay, snarling and baring its pointed white teeth. It might well have bitten Chnay had the metal chain around its neck not pulled it short, just inches away from his ankles.

Alerted by the sound, one of the cooks rushed out of the kitchen and grabbed Chnay's arm. Chnay struggled, trying to twist free, as the cook yelled for help.

From the other direction, the tall bare-chested man appeared. "What's going on?" he demanded.

Scared, I tried to run past him, but he caught me by the wrist.

"Who are you?" he growled, bending down to look at me. The white crescent-shaped object dangling from his chain, I saw now, was a huge tiger's tooth. He shook me by the arm, roughly. "What're you up to?" he asked.

I opened my mouth, but no sound came out.

"They were trying to steal food, sir," the cook said, still hanging on to Chnay.

"Stealing food? How dare they steal from Kung Silor?" the man with the tiger tooth demanded.

I swallowed hard. So this was the leader of the base camp. We couldn't have gotten into worse trouble if we had tried.

"Well? Answer me!" he thundered.

I could tell by the stricken look on Chnay's face that he wasn't going to be any help. I slipped my free hand into my pocket and took out my magic marble. Please, I begged it silently, please give me courage. Make me strong, and brave. The marble felt heavy and smooth in my fist, and as I held it, I felt it radiate a kind of power.

I took a deep breath, and felt calmer. "I'm sorry, Mr. Kung, sir," I managed to say. "But we were hungry."

"That doesn't mean you can steal my food," Kung Silor said sternly.

Well, how else would we have gotten it, I thought. To my horror, I found that I had spoken the thought aloud. Was that the magic marble at work?

Kung Silor looked taken aback, then amused. "You could have asked for it," he said.

I looked at the drumsticks in Chnay's hand. A trickle of oil dripped off them. At that moment I felt I wanted a piece of chicken more badly than I had ever wanted anything. Impulsively, I took one of the drumsticks from Chnay, then turned to Kung Silor. "Fine, I'll ask for it, then. Can I have it, please?" I said.

The cook gasped. "Insolent brat!" he hissed, and made a move to grab me.

Kung Silor waved him aside. He studied me with new interest. "I like you, little girl," he said. "You've got spirit."

"My name's Dara," I told him. "And I'm not little."

"All right, Dara, I'll let you off this time. But don't let me catch you stealing any more food, or I'll have your mother whip you."

"Yes, sir," I said. My instincts told me not to reveal that I didn't know where my mother or any of my family were.

He started to turn away, dismissing us all with an absentminded wave.

"Sir," I called out, "about that piece of chicken . . ."

"Yes, yes," he said impatiently. "Take it."

"Thank you, sir," I said. "But could we have some rice with it, too, please?"

He laughed, a deep throaty sound. "Anything else you want, Dara?" he said.

I squeezed the marble for good luck. "I'd like to work in the kitchen," I said quickly. "In exchange for free meals."

Kung Silor looked at the cook. "Well, could you use her? How about it?"

The cook glared at me. "If you say so, sir," he said reluctantly. He released Chnay and stalked back into the kitchen.

When we were left to ourselves again, Chnay looked at me with something close to awe.

"Kung Silor is right," he said. "You've got spirit."

I smiled, but I knew it was actually the magic that Jantu had put in the marble.

12

The next day I was kept busy in the kitchen with chores assigned me by the cook. All morning I scrubbed pots so thickly encrusted with soot that my arms were aching long before I was through. Then, after a brief break for lunch, I was told to peel a huge basket piled high with garlic. Only when dinner was quietly simmering on the rows of stoves did I have a quiet moment to myself.

Taking the plate of rice and stew the cook had ladled out for me, I retreated to a corner of the kitchen where the cook had had me sleep the night before. Chnay had promised me that he would spend the day looking around for my family, and I had been waiting impatiently for him to bring me news. But there had been no sign of him.

I had finished almost all the rice on my plate before I noticed that the monkey was watching me, its bright, black-rimmed eyes unblinking. Taking a handful of rice, I offered it to the monkey. It did not move.

"Well, go on, take it," I said. "I won't hurt you if you won't hurt me." I tossed the rice at the monkey. It edged forward, its chain clinking behind it, and snatched up the lump of rice, skittering back into the shadows before eating.

I laughed. "You know, I don't mind what you did to us last night," I said, glad to have somebody to talk to. "In fact, I guess I should be grateful. Otherwise I wouldn't be eating so well." The monkey cocked its head, as if listening intently.

"I haven't had much to eat for days now," I said.

"You know how it is. If you don't have a family, nobody bothers to feed you." I tossed another lump of rice at the monkey, closer this time. The little monkey came forward and ate it right there, without retreating to its corner.

"I wonder how you lost your family? You look like you need a mother yourself. You're just a baby, really, aren't you?" I had seen how baby monkeys clung on to their mother's fur, as the mothers swung from tree to tree in the forest. "Did you fall off one day, and get lost? Or did some soldiers shoot your mother, and bring you back here?"

It crept even closer, and I held out the last bit of my rice. "Poor thing, you're all alone now, aren't you?" The monkey came up to me and took the rice right from my hand. Its paw was leathery and padded. As it daintily ate the rice, I reached out and stroked its furry wrist.

The shadows lengthened into night, and still Chnay did not come. Only when it was pitch-dark, and the full moon risen high above the tallest sugar palm tree, did he finally show up.

Before he would tell me anything, he nagged me into getting him a plate of leftover rice. I slipped into the kitchen storage room and got some rice and pork rind for him.

"I didn't find them yet, but I think they're definitely here," Chnay said, crunching noisily on his pork rind. "I found out there's a whole other section on the northern edge of the base camp that we never explored. They're probably there."

"So you'll look there tomorrow?" I asked.

"Why should I? They're your family." Chnay scowled, and for a moment he seemed like the mean, tough bully who used to smash our toys.

I hesitated, biting my lips. "Please?" I asked,

adding, "There will be pork and basil leaf for dinner tomorrow night."

Chnay smiled, and his face softened. "Fine. I'll keep looking if you will keep feeding me," he said.

I considered this for a while, then nodded. "That sounds like a good idea," I said. And then, picking up his empty plate, I went back into the kitchen for another helping of rice for him.

After that, so promptly would Chnay show up for his dinner every night that I suspected he had been waiting in the shadows for some time. I would sneak him out the bowlful of food that I had kept aside, and we would talk as he ate. But he never had any news to report.

On the third evening, I refused to give him any food. "How do I even know you're really searching for them?" I demanded. "You could have just fooled around all day, and then come here for your free dinner."

Chnay took a look at me and turned away. "If that's the way you feel, I might as well leave right now," he said quietly. There was none of the bluff and swagger in his voice that I had seen in him before, only a kind of disappointment. Without another word, he started walking away.

"Wait, don't go!" I said, pulling him back to his usual spot under the palm tree. "I'll get your dinner. What do you want? Cabbage stew or salted fish?"

"Both," he said promptly, and sat down.

"I was at the square all day," Chnay said as he spooned some cabbage into his mouth. "Watching the new recruits practice marching around the flagpole. There are thousands of newly recruited soldiers due to swear allegiance to the Khmer Serei flag. I hear all sorts of ministers and officials have been invited, too, and there'll be a huge banquet after the flag-raising ceremony . . ."

"What do I care about some stupid ceremony," I said. "I want to find my family!"

"That's why I was at the square," Chnay said patiently. "With everybody standing around watching the drills, I thought I might spot your mother there. And I thought if Sarun was one of those recruits, I might spot him, too."

"Well, did you?"

Chnay paused dramatically. "I thought I saw your brother, or somebody who looked like him, marching around the flagpole."

"You thought? Why didn't you make sure?"

"They were all marching by so fast, I couldn't catch up with him," Chnay said. "But I'll go back tomorrow and look again."

I took a deep breath. "Are you just making this up?" I demanded. "Or do you really think you saw Sarun?"

"I wouldn't lie to you," he said. "Not even for cabbage stew and salted fish every night."

The next day I could not keep my mind on my chores in the kitchen. It took me twice as long to scrub the pots, because I would drift into a daydream about finding my family. And that afternoon the cook had to yell at me three times before I heard him. When I hurried over to him, he was in a foul mood.

"Pay attention," he snapped. "I don't know why I even bother with you, a skinny little orphan like you." He glowered at me.

"I'm not an orphan," I said.

"Well, you're little, and you sure are skinny. But I guess I need all the help I can get. Well, don't just stand there, child. Let's go!" Impatiently he beckoned me to follow him out of the kitchen.

Obediently I trailed after him as he walked out of the kitchen and down a narrow path past Kung Silor's quarters. We crossed the bamboo bridge over the trench. The path widened and then opened out toward the parade grounds.

People were bustling about, hammering planks to make a large wooden platform for a stage. Loudspeakers had been strapped onto the palm trees, and marching songs were being played over the air. Hundreds of women and ragged children stood at the edge of the parade ground, gazing at the soldiers.

Marching in elaborate formations around the flagpole were the soldiers. Dressed in the dappled green of jungle fatigues, they looked deadly serious, each with a gleaming rifle jutting from his shoulder.

Quickly I scanned their faces. They seemed so grim and fierce that I was almost afraid of finding Sarun among them.

"What're you standing there for? Hurry up, I don't have all day!" the cook snapped. He walked on ahead, skirting around the square, toward a path on the opposite side.

"It's hard enough feeding the general and his staff," he grumbled, walking so quickly that I had to run just to keep up with him. "Now I'm supposed to feed the new recruits, too? Just because their rice rations have run out, I have to get more rice for them?"

"Where're we going?" I asked.

He ignored me and kept on walking. I followed him to the opposite side of the square.

It was quieter here, as the spectators seemed to be confined to the other side. The cook veered off and headed toward a low thatched shed that looked as if it had been hastily built. As I approached, I instantly recognized the sound that was coming from this shed: it was rice being pounded. Dum-dedum-dum-dedum. The steady rhythm of wooden poles pounding at mortars of unhusked rice grains was something I had grown up with and always liked. In the midst of this army camp, against the background of marching songs and loud military orders, the pounding sounded reassuringly familiar.

I remembered the clever toy mobile that Jantu had made, with the dolls of two village women pounding rice. Playing with the toy had reminded me of home and made me happy. Now, with the pounding of real rice-husking in that shed, how much closer I felt to home! I looked up at the cook expectantly. "Do you want me to help pound rice?" I asked him.

"Just winnow it. Here." He picked up a round rattan tray by the side of the shed and handed it to me. "You know how, don't you?"

I nodded and took the rattan tray from him. This would be more fun than scrubbing pots, I thought. I had always liked flicking the full tray of rice grain, watching the white grain and brown husks fly up into the air, and catching the heavier grains as they rained down.

We walked into the shed, and I saw six women working in pairs inside. Each woman held a thick wooden pole and would pound a mortar filled with rice as her partner lifted her pole and waited her turn. It was dim, and dusty with the powdery rice bran, but the air was fragrant and warm. Along the back wall of the shed were stacks of bulging gunnysacks.

The cook guided me over to a corner and pointed to a mound of rice that had already been pounded, the brown husks split off from the white grain inside. I knew what I was expected to do.

Scooping up the hulled grain from that mound

into my tray, I started tossing the rice up, forcing the lighter rice husks up and out of my tray. It had been a long time since I had winnowed rice, and I enjoyed doing it again. The cook watched me for a minute and nodded in approval, before turning away to leave.

Just then one of the women lifted one of the gunnysacks of rice grain and heaved it over her shoulder. As she started to pour the rice into an empty mortar, I caught a glimpse of the bag. Stenciled in green ink were the words "Rice Seed."

I stared. Rice seed—seeds of the high-yielding, long-grained rice variety that Sarun had so cherished. What these women were pounding in this shed was no ordinary unhusked rice but rice of a special variety, carefully bred and treated, so that each grain, clean and whole, would germinate in the fields back home!

I dropped my rattan tray and ran after the cook. "Wait!" I said, catching up with him. "They shouldn't be doing this."

The cook glared at me but said nothing.

I tugged at his sleeve. "It's a waste," I cried. "They're destroying rice that's meant to be planted, not eaten. Why don't they just use regular rice?"

"We've run out of it, child. With all these new recruits joining up, we've used up our supply of milled rice. And the next distribution of it won't be until after the flag-raising."

I took a deep breath. "But . . . but it's wrong!" I cried. "This is rice for farmers to plant, not for soldiers to eat!"

"Oh, be quiet!" the cook snapped. "Just take a look out there!" Roughly he pulled me to the door and gestured outside. "What do you see? Farmers or soldiers?" he demanded.

I looked. Through the narrow doorway I could see the dusty square, filled with row after precise row of soldiers standing at attention, their guns held stiffly against their shoulders.

"Well, child?" His voice was gentler now, almost sad. "You see anybody who's going to plant your precious rice seed?"

A dozen soldiers marched smartly up to the flagpole and, at some barked command, fired off their guns into the air. The gunfire resonated through the hot dusty afternoon.

I felt as if something had been torn from me, and I ached with the loss of it. Blindly I pushed past him and stumbled into the bright sunlight. No, I thought, not the rice seed, too. That's meant for us, for the women and children, for the harvest next year, for our new lives. Each rice seed, I thought, if it was carefully sown and transplanted, carefully watered and harvested, would yield fifty grains of new rice.

And now? That same kind of rice seed was being pounded and crushed, to feed these men, farmers who had, practically overnight, been turned into soldiers. It didn't make sense, I thought; none of it made any sense.

I had reached the edge of the square, and a contingent of soldiers marched past me, saluting smartly at the flagpole in front of them.

I looked down at my hand. Still cupped in my palm were some broken rice grains, the brown husks stripped off by the pounding, to expose the delicate white grain inside. None of these rice grains would sprout, or grow into tall stalks heavy with plump new rice grains. I remembered my brother's face, how flushed with hope and wonder it was, when he had shown me that first handful of rice seed as we approached the Border. With rice seed like that,

Sarun had said, we could really return to our home in Cambodia and start our lives over.

A soldier marching by bumped against me and knocked the rice out of my hand. I stood back and watched his boots tread the bits of rice into the sand.

When I looked up again, that soldier had marched past. Another soldier marched by me. And another, and another. A seemingly endless series of faces flashed past.

Then I saw Sarun. His eyes straight ahead, his mouth set in a grim line, he marched right by me.

Sarun! I tried to call out to him, but nothing but a hoarse rasp came out.

In step with all the other soldiers, Sarun kept right on marching. In another instant he had turned sharply, and he was soon lost to view among the spectators on the other side of the square.

Stunned, I stood rooted to the spot. Could I have imagined it all? But no—that soldier was my brother.

Abruptly I ran along the edge of the square, trying to catch up with him. Soon I was engulfed in the crowd of onlookers on the other side. I tried to ram and elbow my way through them, but everyone was bigger and taller than I was, and I couldn't budge them.

"Sarun!" I cried. "Sarun! Wait! Sarun!"

Ahead of me, I saw a narrow break in the crowd, and began to make my way to it. Just as I was about to wriggle through, I felt someone grabbing my shoulder, pulling me back. I tried to shake the hand off, but it held on tight. Desperately, I tried to twist free, sobbing my brother's name.

Then, as if in a dream, I heard someone calling my name. The voice was low and gentle, and so full of love that I went limp. Slowly, holding my breath, not daring to hope, I turned around.

My mother opened her arms to me and drew me into them. She was big and warm and soft and she smelled like wet earth after a rainstorm. She held me and rocked me back and forth, back and forth, as if I were a baby again. And as I pressed against her, warmth against warmth and softness against softness, I could feel between us the hard round lump of the magic marble.

Chapter 13

It was the magic marble, I told them, handing the smooth ball of clay to Grandpa Kem as we all sat around the fire that evening. I had just finished telling them everything that had led up to our reunion. I was snuggled against my mother, soaking in the warmth and concern of my family. If only Chnay had agreed to join us for dinner instead of stalking off on his own, I thought with a pang of regret, he might have become part of my family.

Grandpa Kem now held the marble up and squinted at it in the firelight. "Looks like any clay marble to me," he said. "You sure it wasn't just plain old good luck that brought you back to us?" He smiled and handed the marble over to Sarun.

"It was good thinking, not good luck," Sarun countered as he took the marble. "She reasoned that she would find us back at the stone beam, and when she didn't, she and Chnay reasoned that we must have gone to Kung Silor's army camp for protection. After that, it was just a matter of time before we met up. That's all," he said, winking at me as he passed the marble to my mother without even glancing at it.

"You make it sound so simple," my mother said, taking the marble. "What about my prayers, all those nights I lay awake praying for Dara's safety?" She put her cheek on top of my head and nuzzled my hair. "Maybe it was the 'magic' marble, or maybe it was the Lord Buddha answering my prayers—what does it matter as long as you're back?"

She handed the marble over to Nea, who was sitting next to us.

"What do you think, Nea?" I asked her. "Is it a magic marble?"

Nea weighed the marble in her hand before answering. "Magic has a way of working for those who believe in it," she said slowly. "Maybe it wouldn't have been magic for someone else, but you were brave and patient, Dara, and you believed in the marble, so maybe the magic worked for you."

As she handed the marble back, she smiled at me. "Anyway, sister, I'm happy you're back with us," she said.

"Sister." Nea had called me sister. I took the marble from her and held it tightly. Was she just being affectionate, or did she mean something more? I looked at her, trying to read her smile. "I'm glad to be back, too . . . sister," I said, using the last word pointedly.

Around me, the others laughed. "Have you guessed, then?" Sarun asked.

"What?" I asked, squeezing the marble. Let it be true, I begged silently. Let Nea become my sister-in-law.

"That Nea and I plan to get married soon?"

It worked! I burst into a delighted grin. No doubt about it, there was powerful magic in this marble. It felt hard and compact in my hand and even seemed a bit heavier now. It didn't matter if no one else quite believed in it. I was sure it had guided me back to the stone beam, helped me find my family, and, in some mysterious way, even linked Sarun and Nea.

Carefully I pocketed the marble, then smiled at Sarun and Nea. Their hands were linked—just like our little clay dolls', I thought. It was all happening just the way Jantu had hoped. They would get married, and our two families would all be together, living in airy, newly thatched houses by the side of the lake. Together we would sow our rice seed in the rainy season, and together harvest the fields when it turned cool. We would be surrounded by babies and bountiful harvests and peace and laughter.

"Wait till I tell Jantu!" I said gleefully. "Let's go to Khao I Dang and get her tomorrow."

"What's the rush?" Sarun asked. "There's plenty of time yet."

"But it's been over a week since I've seen Jantu," I blurted out indignantly. "I want to make sure Baby's all right!"

"I'm sure he's fine," Sarun said placatingly. "Khao I Dang is one of the most protected refugee camps around here. Besides, you can't go rushing off to see them. It's too far away to walk to, and you'd need a special pass to ride on one of the trucks or vans that go back and forth between Nong Chan and Khao I Dang."

"How do we get the special pass?" I asked.

"I'll have to ask my commanding officer," Sarun said, sticking out his chest. "It'll probably take time."

"Not too much time, I hope," Nea said quietly. "The monsoon rains are starting. If we want to prepare the seedbeds and get the rice seed sown, we'll have to leave very soon." She passed him the platter of fried banana fritters she had prepared as a special treat for this reunion dinner, and helped him to the crispiest fritter. "We should get Jantu out and then start for home as soon as possible. Or we may miss the planting season altogether."

"The planting season?" Sarun echoed, as if he was mystified about what it was. "I can't think about planting seasons now. I've got more important things to consider."

"Like what?" I asked.

"The flag-raising, of course. It's only twelve days away," he said, his mouth full of banana. "I'm going to be marching in it, doing complex drills before the Prince."

Although he hadn't enlisted in Kung Silor's army, Sarun explained, he had volunteered to take part in the special drills, and would have to train every day.

I listened as Sarun also described, eyes glowing, how he had learned to load a gun and take aim. "You have to know how to sight the target," Sarun said, demonstrating with the rifle he had kept propped against him. He cocked his head and in deadly earnest squinted down the length of the gun. He suddenly looked so severe and belligerent that I was unnerved.

I thought of the way he had looked marching in the square that afternoon, his shoulders back, his head high, his mouth set, looking as if he had been a soldier all his life. And I suddenly realized, with a sinking feeling in my heart, that he had been enjoying himself. My brother liked being a soldier.

"What about the special pass for us to go to Khao I Dang?" Nea asked him now. "Will you ask for it tomorrow?"

Sarun frowned. "Don't rush me," he said. "I'll get around to it." He took the last fritter off the plate and stuffed it into his mouth.

There was nothing left on the platter except a few crumbs. Sarun had not even thought to pass the platter around, let alone leave anyone else a fritter or two. I reached over and took one of the crumbs. It was sweet and crunchy, and still slightly warm.

The next morning, Nea and I watched Sarun go off to his military practice. Silhouetted against the morning light, he reminded me of the times he used to go off to the paddy fields at dawn, a hoe on his shoulder. The only difference was that instead of a hoe there was now a gun.

As he disappeared into the forest, Nea sighed. It was a small, discouraged sound. "He's changed, hasn't he?" she said.

I nodded gloomily.

"I remember when I first met him," Nea continued wistfully. "He was always talking about planting a good rice crop and fishing in the lake . . ."

"I know," I said, thinking of how Sarun had told Nea how nice our village was, the day he had come back from his first mass distribution.

"He never talks about that anymore. All he seems to care about now is war and weapons, how to plant land mines, when target shooting is, how to march around in formation."

"Can't you tell him you want to go back home, to the farming, soon?"

"I've tried, Dara. There's even a caravan leaving for Siem Reap in about two weeks, and I had wanted to join it. But when I asked Sarun about it, he got angry."

"Then get angry back at him. Tell him you want—"

"I can't, Dara. I don't want to fight with him. He's going to be my husband. And besides, he said we could go on the next caravan . . ."

"Sure, or the next one, or the next one," I retorted. "At this rate, we'll be too late. If we don't make it back soon, how will we have time to plow the land and sow the rice seed?"

Nea sighed. "I don't know, Dara," she said dejectedly. "There's nothing we can do about it."

I thought for a moment. "Yes there is," I said. "We could make the preparations for leaving now—clean and oil the oxcarts, load them up, and then pick up

Jantu, all in time to join the caravan."

Nea stared at me incredulously. "All by ourselves?" she whispered. "Without telling Sarun?"

"He doesn't need to know. And he probably wouldn't be interested, anyway," I answered.

"But do you realize how heavy each sack of rice is?" Nea asked.

"We can back the carts right up to the tents where the sacks are stored," I countered quickly.

"And do you know how many sacks there are?"

"We will stack them up carefully, so the cart doesn't get lopsided."

"And what about the tools, and the nets?"

"Of course, we would have to spread the tarp over everything, and strap it down with good thick rope."

"And what about the carts? They're not even cleaned, or oiled. Our rear wheel was already creaking badly on our way here."

"We'll just have to grease the axle," I said.

"Do you know how?" Nea demanded.

"I'll learn."

Nea shook her head. "No. There's no way we could possibly do all that."

I jutted my chin at her defiantly. "We can, and we will," I said.

Frowning, Nea looked at me as if she were seeing me for the first time. "You've changed, too, Dara," she said slowly. "You didn't use to be this . . . this . . ."

"Rude?" I suggested.

Nea smiled. "Either that, or this sure of yourself," she said.

I reached in my pocket and squeezed the magic marble. "Well? Where shall we start? How about with cleaning the oxcarts?"

Nea's laugh was exasperated. "All right," she said. "We might as well give it a try."

That same morning, Nea and I dragged out my family's oxcart and swept it clean of all the broken twigs, straw, and spiderwebs that weeks of neglect had heaped on it. It was good to get on its warped planks again, to feel its rough sides and its smooth wooden wheels.

After we finished cleaning and repairing my oxcart, we did the same for Nea's. Satisfied that both were in good enough condition to make the long trip home, we turned our attention to the oxen. Like the carts, they had been neglected for some time, and looked mangy and dirty.

We led our oxen to one of the deeper mudholes and scrubbed them down there. They seemed to enjoy the water and would twist around and stare at us with their long-lashed eyes, snorting warm moist breaths on us.

"We're going home," I murmured to the smaller ox as I splashed more cool water over him. "You'll be feeling the monsoon rains on your back soon, and churning up the soft mud in the fields again. How about that?" He snorted, and Nea and I laughed.

Cleaning the oxcarts and the oxen kept us pleasantly busy for a few days, but the next step would be trickier. All the supplies we had accumulated during the mass distributions—the sacks of rice grain and rice seed, the hoe heads and rope and fishnets and tarpaulin—would have to be loaded into the oxcarts and then strapped down. This was strenuous work, usually reserved for the men.

Together we backed our oxcarts up to the tent where our sacks of rice and rice seed were stowed. We each grabbed a corner of a sack and lifted.

Half running and half stumbling with the sack of rice held between us, Nea and I headed for one of the oxcarts, probably looking very much like a crab scuttling across the sand. But we managed to reach the cart, and even to swing the sack neatly into it. Nea wiped the sweat off her forehead. "We did it," she said, sounding very surprised.

"I told you we could." I grinned, panting.

Again and again we did this, moving sack after sack from the shelter of the blue tarp and into the wagon. After a while there was a layer two deep of the precious rice-seed bags on the bottom of the oxcart.

If we planted the rice seeds with care and if the weather was good, I knew that the seeds we brought home in the cart would be enough to supply half the village next year. I felt a deep satisfaction that these seeds, at least, would not be broken and crushed to feed the soldiers here.

The next day we hauled the bags of rice grain into the carts, putting them over the rice seed. Eight sacks to a layer, three layers thick, in each of the two carts. At first Mother and Grandpa Kem were reluctant to help, fearing Sarun's anger, but then they took to giving us a hand, too.

After the bags of rice were loaded on, there was still more to be done.

We cleaned the mud and rust off the hoe heads and other tools left lying out in the open behind our shelter. Carefully we packed them in the oxcarts, on top of the rice bags. We washed and dried our clothes and scrubbed our kettle and pots. We gathered straw for the oxen for the trip home. We draped the sheet of blue plastic tarpaulin over everything, to keep things protected and dry. And finally we strapped it down with sturdy rope, double-knotting it.

By the end of it, my back was so sore that it hurt terribly even to stand straight. And Nea said her shoulders felt as if they were on fire.

But when I stood back and looked at the two oxcarts, now piled high with rice grain and rice seed, packed tight with tools and fishnets, covered with the blue tarp, and strapped with strong rope, I felt a surge of satisfaction.

Our timing had been excellent. There were three days left before Sarun's all-important flag-raising, and five before the caravan to Siem Reap would leave. All we had to do now was bring Jantu and Baby back from the hospital at Khao I Dang, wait for Sarun to perform his military rituals at the flag-raising, and then hitch our oxcarts up and drive on home!

Gratefully I held the magic marble in my hand and thanked it for having had things work out so neatly. Nothing, I thought, could hold us back now.

Chapter 14

Nea and I took off a day to rest our sore backs, taking turns to massage each other's neck and shoulders for long stretches during the day. Then, knowing that we could not put off confronting Sarun any longer, we cornered him before he left for his military drills the next morning, his rifle propped on one shoulder.

"We've got something to show you," Nea said, gently guiding him by the elbow to the large tamarind tree where we had parked the oxcarts.

Sarun's jaw dropped in surprise when he saw that our oxcarts were already fully packed and ready to go. "Who did this?" he demanded, his voice low but angry.

"We . . . we did," Nea said evenly. "Now will you ask for the special pass to Khao I Dang?"

"Impossible," Sarun declared. "My commanding officer is very busy. The big flag-raising ceremony is tomorrow, you know. I can't bother him with details like this."

"When will you ask, then?"

"In another week or so," Sarun said carelessly. "At most two weeks."

"Two weeks!" I exclaimed. "I'm not going to wait that long. I'll ask for the passes myself. I know who General Kung Silor is. I'll go ask him."

Sarun looked alarmed. He had been impressed by the story of how I had confronted the general about the roast chicken, and I think he took my threat seriously.

"All right, I'll ask," he finally conceded.

"When?" I persisted.

"Tomorrow," he said. "After the flag-raising."

"No," I said. "Today."

His mouth set in a tight line, he went off in the direction of the officers' tent. Within a few minutes he was back, a sheet of paper in his hand.

"Here," he said, thrusting it at me. "You can take the Red Cross van from the Nong Chan gates to and from Khao I Dang tomorrow."

It was on the tip of my tongue to ask him why he had waited so long to get this special pass, if he could have gotten it so easily. But I was too relieved to be angry, and took the piece of paper from him without a word.

"Can you come with us?" Nea asked him.

Sarun shook his head. "I've just been assigned sentry duty," he said. "It's my big chance. It means I can really shoot with my gun now, instead of just marching around with it."

I eyed his gun warily. "Who are you going to shoot?" I asked.

"The enemy, of course," he answered. "It's my responsibility now to protect the base camp from enemy attacks."

"What enemy attacks?" I demanded. "I haven't seen any—"

Nea put a warning hand on my arm. "Let's not argue with your brother," she murmured, with that careful sweetness edged with caution that one woman uses with another. She reached over to take the special pass away from me. "And thank you for getting this, Sarun," she said. "We'll go tomorrow, then."

"All right," Sarun said grudgingly. "But be sure you come back by nightfall. The forest trails are dangerous in the dark."

"Yes, Sarun," Nea replied meekly. Then she

flashed me a mischievous smile. "Anything you say."

The next morning, Nea and I set off. At the edge of the base camp, Sarun stood guard with two other armed soldiers who were also posted there as sentries, and he saw us off. I looked back at them warily. Leaning against the palm trees, their guns pointing recklessly into the air, they looked ominous—more of a threat than a protection.

The trail through the forest back toward Nong Chan was deeply rutted. A light rain was falling on the forest trail, and the mud path was slippery and laced with deep puddles, making some sections of it almost impassable for oxcarts.

I remembered how, when we had first arrived at the Border, the oxcarts were going the other way, out of Cambodia and westward toward Thailand. Now, with the onset of the monsoon rains, long caravans of oxcarts loaded down with tools and rice seed were going the opposite way, starting on the long trek back toward Cambodia.

As we walked past each caravan, we called out greetings to the families, asking where they were headed. "Battambang," came the exuberant reply from one caravan; or "Siem Reap," from another string of oxcarts; or "Pursat, on the south side of Tonle Sap lake," the team leader of yet another caravan answered.

A creaky old cart rolled toward us, laden with sacks of rice. I saw a girl about my own age standing on the bullock cart, the reins in her hands, as her father walked beside it.

"Turn back, you're going the wrong way! Cambodia's that way!" the girl said, teasingly. "You'd better start for home before it's too late to sow your rice seed!"

"Don't worry, we'll be going home soon, too," I called out as she passed by. Still, I couldn't help but envy her as I watched her drive her laden cart homeward.

The trail improved once we emerged from the forest into the barren fields of Nong Chan. Ever since the fighting had eased off slightly in the last few days, thousands of families had moved back there and were living in their makeshift shelters again.

We threaded our way through the campsites, toward the tall bamboo watchtowers across the fields. There we presented the special pass to the relief officials, certifying that we had a sick relative at the Khao I Dang hospital, whom we were going to see. Only after that document had been thoroughly examined were we allowed to board a white van parked near one of the watchtowers.

I had never been in anything like it before, and it was exciting to be seated next to the driver, where Nea and I had a good view of the dirt road winding into Thai territory toward Khao I Dang camp. Once I got used to the dizzying speed with which the scenery flashed past the window, I watched everything with growing interest. We passed Thai village houses perched on stilts whose thatched roofs rose above the banana groves and the tamarind trees. The houses seemed so prosperous and peaceful that I felt wistful just looking at them. Stretching out on either side of the road were the rice paddies of Thailand, still brown and stubbled with the rice stalks from the past harvest. Already, however, there were patches of vibrant green where rice seedbeds had been sown and sprouted. Farmers were plowing or harrowing the rest of the fields, readying them for the transplanting of the rice seedlings from the small seedbeds into the paddy fields. It was a very familiar scene, and I longed to get home and help start the preparations for our own seedbeds. There was so much to be done before the monsoon rains began in earnest—we really had to go home soon!

I reached in my pocket and touched my magic marble lightly. Just a little more help, that's all I need, I told it. Help me find Jantu, and get us on our way homeward. That's not much to ask, is it?

It was high noon when we finally arrived at the Khao I Dang refugee camp. The camp itself was surrounded by barbed wire fencing, and at the gates were several armed guards. I felt uneasy. Were things that bad within the camp, I wondered, that barbed wire was needed to keep the people inside from escaping?

One of the guards took our special pass and motioned us to get off the van. Politely I explained why we had come, but his reply was curt and incomprehensible. Of course, I thought, he's a Thai—he doesn't speak our language. Sure enough, the guard called out to a young Cambodian nearby, and, giving him our pass, gestured at him to accompany us around the refugee camp.

Entering Khao I Dang camp was like coming into an entirely different world. Everything, absolutely everything, was in perfect order.

Moments before, I had thought the barbed wire was to keep the refugees inside. Now that I was on the other side of the fence, I realized that it was there just as much to keep people like me out. Compared to the swirling confusion of the fields at Nong Chan, this refugee camp was incredibly calm. Almost like stepping into our toy village, I thought.

The streets stretched out in neat rows ahead of me, each one clean and narrow and absolutely straight. Nea and I walked down one of them, gazing at the houses on either side. The houses all looked exactly the same—and even though they were nothing more than mud walls and a thatched roof, still they were new and neat. There were even small vegetable plots growing beside some houses, with melon vines creeping up the doorway. Whoever lived in these houses, I realized with a stab of envy, could count on staying here for a while.

Then I remembered the barbed wire and realized that these people were cooped up here like turtles in a stagnant pond, hoping only to be allowed to emigrate to some cold, distant country. And I was glad I wasn't living there after all.

Slowly I walked down the street, barely aware of Nea and the guard walking ahead. Some reddish dust from the street, stirred up by a passing breeze, settled over my bare arms. Nothing else moved. The sun beat down relentlessly, and there was not a tree in sight. The people must have retreated into the shade of their own houses, since there was nobody around.

We followed the guide through a maze of streets until we reached a huge, empty square with a water tank in the middle of it. A few children played with toy trucks made from rusty tin cans. A young woman sat breast-feeding her baby nearby. Those were the only signs of activity. The guard turned to Nea. "You know which ward your cousin's in?" he asked.

"The . . . the hospital," Nea said hesitantly.

"Yes, but which ward?" the guide repeated irritably. "Pediatric? Surgical? Malnutrition? We've got over ten different wards in the hospital area, you know." He gestured at the long thatched sheds clustered around the far end of the square. Each was the size and shape of the kitchen back at the base camp, but tacked onto each front door was a sign painted with different words and symbols. The signs made each building look very official.

"Which ward? We . . . we don't know," Nea said.

"Well, we'll try the children's ward first," he said, going into one of the sheds and motioning for us to follow him.

It was dim under the thatched roof, and I had to blink away the glare of the sun outside before I could make out what was before me.

It was the silence that first struck me. Row after row of children lay on cots of split bamboo, most of them so thin that, except for their distended stomachs, they looked like frail skeletons draped in loose skins. Too weak even to cry, these children remained completely motionless and silent. Some lay asleep in their mothers' arms; others stared blankly at the bamboo rafters.

As my eyes grew accustomed to the dim light, I saw that clipboards were hanging above each cot, often next to plastic bags dripping blood or clear fluids into thin arms. Stumbling a bit across the dirt floor, I had to stifle an urge to get away, back out into the world of sunlight and calm. But Nea gave me a gentle tug, and together we walked farther down the aisle.

"Mostly malnutrition cases," the guide said over his shoulder. "Although, of course, many of them have dysentery or malaria on top of it."

Long bony arms and legs, swollen bellies, skin flaking off a few of them, hair like straw, and always those huge, unblinking eyes.

"A lot of these children were weak already," the guide was saying to Nea, "but during the escape out of Cambodia, thousands more starved, because of Pol Pot's scorched-earth policy: his soldiers burned the villages' rice supplies just so the invading Vietnamese troops wouldn't get at them."

I thought of my own village and then of Kung Silor's soldiers, fed on rice seed, parading around the flag. How could they do this while countless children inside Cambodia starved to death?

Nea must have been thinking the same thing. In a shaky voice, she asked, "These children . . . why must the children suffer, when it's the men who are fighting?"

The guide shrugged. "What do you think this war is all about, sister?" he said.

I found it was hard to keep walking down the aisle.

Farther down was a boy who was older than the others. So thin that he seemed little more than a shadow, he might have been about my age, but he couldn't have weighed much more than Jantu's chubby baby brother. His face already looked like a skull, and his eyes were dark and sunken, though strangely glistening.

"Malaria, dysentery, and of course severe malnutrition," the guide said, glancing at the clipboard. "He doesn't have long. Three days, maybe four."

His grandmother, who was cradling him, ignored us and, slowly unbuttoning her shirt, very gently drew the boy's head toward her wrinkled breasts. He nuzzled there, and closed his eyes. Crooning, she held him close and rocked him.

Finally we were at the end of the long aisle, and I felt both sad and relieved: it was a terrible place, but at least Jantu and Baby weren't there.

The guide had gone on ahead and was waiting for us outside. "Do you have any idea where else your cousin might be?" he asked.

Nea shook her head, looking slightly dazed.

"Well, there's the surgical ward next door," he

said. "You could try looking in there." He hesitated by the door, then held it open for us. "You go ahead. I'll wait for you out here."

As soon as I entered the ward, I understood why the guide chose to remain outside. It was even worse than the first shed.

Dark and gloomy, the long room was crowded with maimed people, some with their legs in plaster casts, others with bloodied gauze wrapped around their heads or chests, still others with their legs strung up to some strange metal pulleys dangling from the rafters. Many had stubs where their arms and legs should have been, the stubs wrapped in gauze stained with blood and pus. Flies swarmed around the wounds, and their buzzing merged with the soft moans of the patients. The air was filled with the smell of urine and vomit.

I took one look and turned right around. "Let's go," I whispered to Nea. "Jantu couldn't be here."

"Let's just take a quick look," Nea insisted.

Reluctantly I followed her. Slipping my hand into my pocket to hold on to the clay marble, I started down the middle aisle, peering into each face as I passed by.

Halfway across the long room, I heard someone calling my name. "Dara! At last! You're here!"

Startled, I spun around.

There stood Jantu in the middle of the shed, looking strong and healthy among all the frail, maimed patients. She waved excitedly at me.

My laugh was one of sheer relief. "Jantu!" I yelled, and ran toward her. It was so wonderful to see her that I grabbed her by the waist and hugged her hard. Nea joined us and shook Jantu's shoulders in delight, as if making sure she was real.

"And where's Baby?" I asked. "Is he all right?"

For answer, Jantu pointed to a cot farther down the aisle. Her baby brother was sitting there, playing with some rubber bands. There was a thick scar running down his ankle and along one foot, but otherwise he looked fine.

"They had to cut his foot open to take out a piece of shrapnel, but it's all healed now," Jantu said. "Come on, take a look for yourself."

We walked over to the baby, and with a joyful coo, Nea reached down and picked him up.

"Why did you take so long?" Jantu was asking me. "What happened? How's everybody? Did you find them at the stone beam?"

"Nobody was at the stone beam," I said, "but I managed to find them." And I told Jantu the rest of the story as she listened breathless and wide-eyed.

As soon as Nea left with Baby to make arrangements for us to leave, Jantu asked, "And Sarun and Nea—they're still . . . together?"

"More than just 'together,'" I said, grinning. "They're getting married."

"Getting married," Jantu repeated, in an awed whisper. Her eyes were glowing. "Just like we had dreamed. So I was right! Sometimes if we dream hard enough, those dreams can shape our lives."

As if in a reverie, she dropped down to sit on the cot next to Baby's.

"Careful! Don't touch it—it hurts enough already!" a hoarse voice broke in.

Jantu looked startled and edged over to the side of the bed. "I'm sorry, Duoic," she said. "Did I hurt you?"

The gaunt figure lying on the cot smiled faintly at her. He was about thirteen or fourteen years old, with thick tousled hair and big eyes. I saw with horror that both his legs were missing, ending in bandaged stubs just above where the knees should have been. The bandages were encrusted with bloodstains and dried pus, and a few flies buzzed around them.

He saw me looking at him, and grunted. "You must be Dara, right?" he asked me.

I nodded shyly.

"Jantu has talked so much about you, but I was beginning to think you were something out of one of her stories." Despite his haggard look, a glint of mischief sparkled in his eyes, and I found myself smiling at him.

"I'm real, all right, Duoic," I said. "It just took us a while to get here."

We got to talking after that. Matter-of-factly, Duoic told me how he had lost touch with his family during their escape from Cambodia. "It was at night. I was holding on to my brother's hand when we heard some soldiers patrolling in the forest in front of us. Mother told us to hide, so we crouched in the bushes for the rest of the night. The next morning I couldn't find any of the others anymore. I panicked, and ran about shouting and looking for them." Duoic paused and frowned. "Then I guess I stepped on one of those land mines planted near the Border, and well . . . here I am."

He reached out and ran his finger across one of his bandaged stubs. There was no smile on his gaunt face now. "Jantu's lucky," he said softly. "She's got you to take her home. Me, I'll be here until . . . until . . ." He shrugged and took a deep breath. For a moment his bony chest seemed thicker, more substantial. Then he let out the air, and his chest caved in again. "Sometimes I don't know why I keep on living," he said.

I did not know what to reply, so I said nothing.

Jantu, however, had taken his hand and was tugging at it gently. "That's no way to talk," she said, almost angrily. "You'll get better. How many times have I told you before: You're strong, you can make it. You've just got to keep trying!"

"Easy for you to say," Duoic mumbled. "You're healthy, and you're leaving."

"But you'll get better. You can be up and around on crutches soon."

For a moment the boy did not reply. He stared blankly at the thatched ceiling above him, and it was as if his face were hardening into an expressionless mask. Then he swallowed and whispered, "I'm thirsty." He looked at me, and his eyes were so sunken they were like tiny pinpoints of light at the end of a tunnel. "Get my water bottle for me, please," he said, pointing under his cot.

I saw a plastic bottle under his cot and reached for it. But before I could pick it up, Jantu stopped me.

"Get it yourself, Duoic!" she said sharply. "You can do it. You almost reached it yesterday."

When I started to protest, Jantu cut me short. "Go on," she told Duoic. "Get the water yourself."

"You get it," he begged Jantu.

"No. You can do it."

He seemed to shrink into the bed. "It's too hard," he said.

Jantu bent down so that her face was up against his. "Try!" she whispered.

The boy turned his face away from her. "I don't want to," he whispered, so softly that it sounded like the faintest breeze in the rushes. "I can't."

"You can," Jantu said, her own whisper fierce and insistent. "Go on, try it. You can do it."

"No."

"Try it!"

For a long moment the boy did not move. Then, taking such a deep breath that he seemed to grow before our very eyes, he started to hoist himself up with his arms. Inch by inch he dragged himself to the side of his bed, then slowly groped under the cot for the water bottle. Finally, with a tremendous effort, he grasped the bottle and pulled it up. Beads of sweat glistened on his forehead, but a small, triumphant smile lit his face.

"I did it," he said.

"I knew you could," Jantu said simply. She looked at him in silence for a long moment, then blurted out, "I've got to go pack now." Abruptly she got up and turned to the other cot, where she started thrusting her baby brother's few clothes into a bundle. Her movements were jerky, almost angry. "Good luck, Duoic," she said gruffly, without looking at him.

"Good luck yourself," Duoic echoed, then added softly, "And don't cry, silly. You should be happy."

I looked carefully at Jantu then, and although she kept her face carefully averted from us, I caught a glimpse of the tears glistening on her cheeks as, without a word, she strode down the aisle toward the door.

Chapter 15

In single file, we walked along the narrow trail through the forest behind Nong Chan, on our way back to the base camp. The same van which had given us a lift to Khao I Dang that morning had taken us back to the Nong Chan gates. We were all tired and subdued, and for the most part we walked in silence, taking turns holding the baby.

By the time we had threaded our way across refugee campsites scattered on the plain at Nong Chan, it was early twilight, and walking into the forest was like entering a sort of green gloom. The last slats of afternoon sunlight shimmered on the puddles of the rutted path. I could barely see Jantu's footprints on the moist soil ahead of me.

"Let's stop for a rest," Nea suggested behind me. "And let me take Baby for a while, Jantu."

"You sure?" Jantu asked. "He's heavy."

For answer, Nea held out her arms. Jantu untied the checkered cloth in which the baby was secured to her, and with a small sigh of relief handed him over to Nea.

As Nea deftly tied the baby's cloth across her chest, adjusting his position so that he straddled her hip comfortably, Jantu walked over to me and put her arm around my shoulders.

"What are you thinking about?" she asked me gently. As ever, she always seemed able to sense it whenever I felt sad.

"Duoic," I answered quietly. "I wish he could have come with us."

"He wouldn't have made it," Jantu said bluntly.

"I suppose not," I said, and sighed. "It's just that . . . it's strange, I had thought that if we could go home and live together, life would be perfect. But now that we're so close to doing that, I feel sad, not happy."

"Because of Duoic?"

"And all the others like him, who won't ever be able to go home again. Why should we be able to pack up and go home when he can't?"

"Duoic doesn't mind my leaving, you know," Jantu said quietly. "He kept saying that it made him happy to think of me going back to a village to grow rice and fly kites and live out a peaceful, normal life. He wouldn't have wanted me to be trapped on the Border, like him."

"Still, it just doesn't seem fair," I said.

"Life isn't fair," Jantu said.

I thought of the Thai villages we had caught a glimpse of on the road outside Nong Chan. They had probably been there for hundreds of years without once being touched by war. No bombs were ever dropped on their paddy fields. None of their men were ever herded off to work camps. Nobody had ever been taken to the nearby forest in the depth of night, and clubbed to death. Nobody had had their legs blown off walking across a field.

"You know, if for some reason I couldn't go home with you all," Jantu mused, "I'd feel the same way Duoic did. I'd want everyone else to go on home without me. Wouldn't you?"

I frowned. The thought of leaving Jantu behind made me feel awful.

"Hey, what is all this gloomy talk?" Nea broke in, chidingly. "Come on, let's go. It's getting dark."

It was true. The twilight was turning to dusk, and soon the trail would be completely swallowed up in darkness. And we were still a good hour away from the camp.

We walked on in silence until, at a clump of wild red ginger under a big ficus tree, we came to a split in the road. Jantu stopped and looked back at us for guidance. I hadn't noticed any fork on the trail on our way out, and was not sure which path we should take now. Nea was looking uncertain, too.

"It's the one on the right, isn't it?" Nea asked me.

"I thought it was the one on the left," I said.

"Sarun said something about one of them leading to a different base camp," Nea said, "and to make sure not to take that one."

"Why not?" Jantu asked.

"Because they're our enemies," Nea said.

"But I thought the Vietnamese soldiers were the enemies," Jantu said.

"Or the Khmer Rouge," I added. "You know, Pol Pot's soldiers."

"Well, they are, too," Nea said vaguely. "But so are the people in the camps right next to ours. Sarun explained it all to me this morning, but I didn't get it too clear."

"I don't think he's too clear on it himself," I said. "He just likes the idea of having lots of enemies, now that he's been given his own gun."

"Well, he did say that if we took the wrong road, we might get shot at," Nea said nervously.

"Sounds as if we're liable to get shot at whichever road we take." Jantu snorted. "Well, do we take the right or the left?"

"The right," Nea said.

"The left," I said at the same instant.

Jantu looked at us both and laughed. "Why don't I decide?" she said. "Let's take this one." And she led us down the left fork.

The light was almost gone by now, and I could tell from Jantu's quickened steps that despite her attempt to be cheerful, she was nervous, too.

As I hurried after her, I put my hand in my shirt pocket and groped for the clay marble. It was still there, reassuringly solid. With it held tight in my fist, I felt a little better.

"I don't think this is the right way after all," I said. I looked at the clusters of ferns laced with wild clematis vines that bordered the path, and felt uneasy. "I don't remember seeing these on the way out," I said, and found that I was whispering. It was very quiet, and the forest seemed thicker and more overgrown than I had remembered. The camp was nowhere in sight.

"Let's turn back," Jantu said.

The baby whimpered, but when Nea tried to soothe him, he started to cry. The noise seemed very loud in the quiet jungle.

"Here, give him back to me," Jantu said.

"It's all right. I can—"

Just then a shot rang out, ripping apart the shroud of silence around us.

"Get down!" I shouted, and threw myself onto the ground. Nea screamed. With all my might, I grabbed her ankle and pulled her and the baby down to the ground with me.

Another shot pierced the air, even nearer this time. Nea was sobbing, her hands clutching wildly at me. I could not see Jantu anywhere.

Voices shouted at us, at first faint, then advancing closer. "Identify yourselves!" someone yelled. "Answer or we'll shoot!"

I felt a stab of shock, colder than any fear. One of the voices was Sarun's.

"Show yourself!" Sarun shouted again, just in

front of us.

"It's Sarun!" Jantu shouted, running forward.

There was another shot. I heard Jantu gasp, a strangled little sound. Slowly she sank to her knees.

Even in the dusk, I could see the blood seeping through the white of her blouse. But she seemed not to notice it. There was a look of bewilderment on her face. "Wasn't that Sarun's voice?" she asked me.

The curtain of tangled vines and leaves parted, and three men burst out, each thrusting a gun at us.

"Sarun!" Nea sobbed.

Sarun stared at her, then swiveled around at the other two sentries. "Who fired that shot?" he demanded.

"I did. They refused to identify themselves, and . . ."

Sarun shook his head in disbelief. "You stupid fool!" he hissed.

"What's going on?" the other soldier asked. "You know these people?"

Before Sarun could answer, Jantu groaned. She touched her chest, then lifted her hand and examined it in the dim light. "It's dark and wet," she whispered. "What . . . what is it?" Then she swayed slightly on her knees and crumpled onto the ground.

I reached her first. Her eyes were closed, her breathing ragged. I knelt beside her and gently, my fingers trembling, started to unbutton her blouse.

"Lay her flat, on the ground," Sarun said, kneeling beside me.

As we did so, Jantu's blouse fell open, exposing her delicate collarbones. Below them, on her right side, was a wide gash from which blood was streaming.

"It looks bad," one of the soldiers grunted. "We should take her to the Khao I Dang hospital."

"What, and risk having all of us shot on the way?" the other soldier asked.

Sarun frowned. "He's right," he said after a moment's hesitation. "It'd be too dangerous now, in the dark. Besides, it's too far away. Better to take her back to the base camp, and get her onto a truck or van tomorrow morning."

I had been trying to stanch the flow of blood on Jantu's chest with a handful of leaves. I looked up at my brother and shook my head. "Jantu needs help now," I said. "We should get her back to the hospital right away."

"You heard what I said," Sarun said curtly. "It's just too dangerous now. There'll be plenty of vehicles heading out after the flag-raising tomorrow. We'll get her a ride to the hospital on one of them."

"That will be . . ." Too late, I had wanted to say. But Sarun had already turned his back to me and was talking to the other soldiers. I felt a wave of panic building up in me. Then Jantu stirred, and though her breathing was ragged, she managed a faint smile.

"That'd be fine," she said, finishing up my sentence for me. "Maybe by the morning I'll be all right, and won't even need to go back to the hospital. Right, Dara?"

Blood was seeping through the layer of leaves and out between my fingers, where I had clumsily tried to hold them against her wound. "Yes, Jantu," I said softly. "You'll be fine by morning." And I was glad that she closed her eyes then, because otherwise she would have been able to tell that I was lying to her.

Chapter 16

When we got Jantu back to the base camp, my mother tended to her as best she could. By the flickering light of a borrowed kerosene lamp, Mother gently peeled away the wad of leaves I had clamped over the wound, and rinsed the blood away. Exposed on Jantu's chest now was a jagged gash between her right nipple and belly button, where the bullet had ripped into her. The bullet must have still been lodged somewhere inside her, since her back was smooth and unmarked. But when Mother tried to press down gently to see where it was, Jantu moaned so pitiably that she didn't dare probe any further. Instead, she took a clean sarong, ripped it into strips, and bound Jantu's chest with it.

Despite the pain that Jantu obviously felt while her wound was being dressed, she fell into a fitful sleep almost immediately afterward.

I brought over my sleeping mat and curled up on it, and fell asleep lying next to Jantu.

I woke up every time Jantu moaned, and would watch helplessly as she tossed her head fretfully from side to side. Sometimes I would stroke her arm, as if by running my hand up and down her smooth dry skin, I could take away some of her pain.

Several times during the night, I took out the clay marble and prayed that it could restore Jantu's strength and make her well again.

"Just one more time," I begged it silently, holding it tight in my fist. "Make Jantu well, and I will never ask for anything again."

Toward morning, when I tried to calm her down

by putting my hand on her cheek, I noticed how hot she was. In alarm, I called my mother and Nea over, but there was little they could do other than put cool, damp rags on her forehead.

Jantu's fever abated as dawn broke, but her face still looked flushed. As Nea bent over to change the damp rag on her forehead, Jantu woke up and blinked sleepily. Her eyes wandered over the thatched palmetto roof of the shelter, then rested on me. She brightened, and for a moment a shadow of her old cocksure grin flashed across her face.

"Dara! You're really here," she murmured. "So I didn't dream it all." She tried to get up, and her smile changed abruptly to a grimace of pain. Bewildered, she glanced down at her chest and saw the sarong strips wound tightly around it. Splotches of blood had seeped through the cloth and stained it a rusty brown. She started to take a deep breath, then stopped when she realized how much even that pained her. Dumbly she looked at me in appeal.

"You're hurt, Jantu," I told her. "Don't try to get up."

"What happened? Tell me," she demanded in a hoarse whisper.

And so, as simply as I could, I told her how Sarun and two other sentries had mistaken us for enemies in the dark, and fired at us, accidentally wounding her. But she was going to get well, I told her quickly. As soon as the flag-raising was over that morning, we would get her on one of the many vehicles that had made their way to the base camp, and get her back to the hospital. She would get proper medical treatment there, I assured her. She would recover quickly, and then we would all go home on our oxcarts, just as we had planned.

As I talked, I watched her anxiously, and it was as

if a mask had descended on her face, making it blank and hard. With a stab of dread, I realized that I had seen the same mask settle on Duoic's face the day before, when he had refused to reach for the water bottle. It was the look of someone who wasn't going to try anymore.

"You *will* get better, Jantu," I said desperately.

For answer, Jantu only closed her eyes. There were dark green shadows under them, and her cheekbones seemed to jut out more sharply. I watched her bandaged chest rise and fall, and it seemed that her breathing had become even more shallow and ragged.

Sarun came into the shelter, ducking his head under the thatched eaves. "How is she?" he asked, in a cheerful voice that seemed to fill up the whole room.

Nea, who was sitting nearby, shushed him and motioned him to go back out, following him out as she did so. Through the thin thatched walls, I heard their whispered conversation.

Nea wanted to try to find a vehicle to get Jantu to the hospital now, but Sarun insisted that there was nothing he could do, that nobody would be leaving until after the flag-raising, which would be over in a few more hours anyway.

"I've got to go march in it," he said impatiently. "You're coming to watch, aren't you? You promised you would." It wasn't a question but a demand.

Nea must have recognized the peremptory tone in Sarun's voice, for after a moment's hesitation she agreed.

"How about the others?" Sarun was demanding now. "Mother and Dara and Grandpa Kem? Weren't they all supposed to come, too?"

I leaned out the opening of the shelter, and said, "I'm not going. I'm staying with Jantu."

Jantu's eyes flickered open at the sound of her own

name, and she said weakly, "No, you go along. I'll be fine."

But I could be as stubborn as my brother, and I insisted that I wasn't going anywhere. In any case, Sarun didn't seem to care much one way or the other whether I would watch him parade around the square. I guess it was really just the grownups, especially Nea, that he wanted to impress.

And so, to humor Sarun, it was agreed that Nea and my mother would go along to the flag-raising, leaving Grandpa Kem behind to do some chores, and to keep us company.

"We'll be back as soon as the flag-raising ceremony is over," Nea told Jantu gently, brushing away a wisp of hair from her cousin's eyes.

"Don't worry, I'll be fine," Jantu said. "But before you go, could you move me into the hammock outside?" she asked Sarun. "I want to be under the open sky. I can't seem to breathe properly in here."

And so Sarun lifted her up in his arms and carefully laid her in the hammock. I saw how much it pained her to be moved, even though she tried not to show it.

Once she was settled into the hammock, however, she looked happier and more relaxed.

Nea and Sarun and Mother left the two of us with the baby, as Grandpa Kem wandered off to gather some straw for the oxen. Jantu waved goodbye to them weakly from her hammock.

It was quiet after they left. The families around us had also gone to watch the ceremony, and we were the only ones around. I leaned back against the tree by Jantu's hammock. Her baby brother was sitting on the ground, scratching circles in the sand with a twig.

"I'll be glad when this flag-raising is over," I said, tugging at the hammock rope gently to get it rocking. "Then Sarun will finally agree to leave, and we can all head home."

Dreamily Jantu watched the canopy of leaves swing by overhead. "Do you really think so, Dara?"

"Of course," I said with forced cheerfulness. "Our carts are packed. The caravan is due to leave in three days. All we have to do is to make you a comfortable nest on top of your cart, and then we'll start driving east."

"I was talking about Sarun," Jantu said. "Do you really think he'll be ready to leave with this caravan?"

"I don't see why not," I said.

"Don't you, Dara? Listen." She gestured in the direction our families had just gone, toward the parade ground.

From the loudspeakers around the square came the sound of strident marching songs. As we listened, the music was replaced by the sound of a voice. It was high-pitched, charged with a fervor clearly designed to be infectious. Long, glib phrases came snaking out of the forest.

"As part of the great revolutionary cause," the voice blared, over the crackling static of the loudspeaker system, "we must wage a struggle against the puppets and lackeys of our enemies. We must strive to be anti-colonialist, anti-Vietnamese, anti-imperialist . . ." The words trailed like paper streamers through the air, fluttering for a moment before being dispersed by the breeze.

"Who was that?" I asked.

"Does it matter?" Jantu said. "They all say the same thing. They seem to think it's a game." Her voice was low and fierce, and she spoke quickly, as if the words had been pent up in her for a long time. "They take sides, they switch sides, they play against each other. Who wins, who loses, whose turn it is to kick next—it's like an elaborate soccer game. Except that they don't use soccer balls. They use us."

Jantu paused, and in the quiet we could hear the voice over the loudspeakers again. "We must keep fighting for the future of Cambodia. We must plant more land mines, arm ourselves with more weapons, fire more bullets—until we kill every last one of the Enemy Number One!" Again there was loud applause.

Jantu smiled. "Look at me," she said gently. "Do I look like your Enemy Number One? And my friend Duoic—whose enemy was he? Oh, Dara, at the hospital I saw so many people brought in, day after day, bleeding and maimed. Most of them weren't even soldiers. Why do they keep shooting at us, Dara? Why?"

I did not know the answer, so I kept silent.

"And the fighting's not going to stop," Jantu went on, her voice low and vehement. "Look what's happening around us. There are far more guns than farm tools being distributed, far more bullets than rice seed. Yet they talk about the future of Cambodia, about rebuilding the country. Does that make any sense to you, Dara?"

Again, I did not know what to say. For a long moment there was only silence. A fly buzzed around Jantu's bandages, alighting on a bloodstain there. I waved it away. "Don't think about such things, Jantu. Just rest up, and everything will be fine."

"Everything will not be fine," Jantu said. "Face it, Dara, things are not going well. I'm not sure that we'll ever make it home."

"Of course we will," I said soothingly. "As soon as

you are well enough to travel, we'll join a caravan and head for home."

Jantu shook her head. "Not even then," she said. "Not even if I get well."

"Why not?"

"Because Sarun won't go."

"Yes he will. We'll make him go," I said.

With great effort, Jantu propped herself up on her elbow on the hammock and looked me right in the eye. "Who will make him?" she asked.

"We will."

Jantu shook her head at me sadly. "Not 'we,' Dara," she said. "You'll have to do it. Alone."

"Why me?"

"Because," she said softly, "I don't think I'll be around to help you."

The rock. That sudden punch of pain, like a rock slamming into my stomach. I recognized that pain from the day of the shelling near the food truck, when Jantu had said, "Lost: we're lost." And now I felt it again, that rock-hard pain.

"No," I whispered. "In just a couple of hours we'll take you to the hospital. You'll get better there."

"Face it, Dara. If you want to go home, you've got to make Sarun leave. I've done all I can. I can't do any more." Her breathing was so shallow that her chest was barely moving. I noticed that fresh blood was seeping through her bandages.

"No," I said. "No."

"Listen to me, Dara. I can't help you anymore. You've got to do the rest."

"No." No, no, please no—in the sudden silence of my fear, I remembered my father's voice the night he was dragged away to be killed in the forest. I had lain there, I had heard the dread and the fear in his voice—and I had felt the fear lodge in my own heart.

Yet he had begged so softly. Was it because he hadn't wanted to wake me up? No, no, no, he had murmured, and as I lay there in the dark, all I could do was to echo in my heart "no." And then there was only the silence.

I felt Jantu's hand on my arm, warm and firm. "Yes, Dara," she was saying. "I know you can do it." She looked at me, her eyes steady and calm.

I pushed the fear and the dread and the voices away, and I tried instead to listen to Jantu's voice, warm and gentle. "Remember when you didn't want to go alone to look for our families, Dara?" she said. "After Baby was wounded? Remember how scared you were then? But you did it, Dara. You went off and found our old campsite, and then you found our families again. You did it, Dara. And you can do it again now."

"But that wasn't me," I said. "It was the magic marble you gave me."

"Magic marble?" A tired smile flickered across Jantu's face. "You really believed in that? In that magic marble?"

"It worked," I said.

"It worked," Jantu said gently, "because you believed it would. That's all."

"Then just make me another one. A bigger one, with stronger magic. I'll believe in that one, too." Desperately I scooped a lump of damp clay from a nearby puddle and tried to give it to Jantu. She wouldn't take it, but I pressed it into her left hand. "Please," I begged her.

Jantu only looked at the lump of clay on her palm, moist and shapeless. Slowly she closed her hand around it, but she made no move to mold it. Except for the sound of her shallow breathing, it was quiet.

I noticed then that she seemed to be having more

trouble breathing. Each breath of air she sucked in seemed to cause her pain. Then, with a great effort, she spoke again. "You've got to believe in yourself, Dara. Not me. Not magic marbles. There's no magic in that marble I gave you, or in this lump of clay in my hand. The magic is only in the making of the marble. You've got to do it on your own."

"Do what?" I asked. "Make my own marble?"

Jantu smiled faintly. "Yes," she said. "Make your own magic marble."

"But, Jantu, I can't. I don't know how. I don't have magic in my fingers the way you do. Please, Jantu, make me one more magic marble. Just one more."

"No," Jantu whispered, and closed her eyes. "You've got to do it yourself." For a long moment there was no sound except the rustling of the leaves overhead.

Jantu looked as if she was about to drift off to sleep, but with an effort she opened her eyes again. "Give me Baby," she told me. "I want to hold him."

I reached down and picked up her baby brother and gently placed him against her left side, where he wouldn't disturb her wound. Tucked against Jantu in the hammock, he gurgled happily. Jantu nuzzled her cheek against his hair and sighed. "Now rock us, Dara," she said quietly. "We're going to sleep."

And so I started to push the cloth hammock, push and swing, to and fro, back and forth. The rhythm of it was soothing.

"Sing to us, Dara," Jantu said softly. "Rock us and sing us to sleep."

I hesitated. "What shall I sing?" I asked.

"Sing about home," Jantu said dreamily. "Home, where we can splash in the paddy fields, and feel the raindrops on our skin, and hear the crickets crying at night . . ." Her voice faded, and she breathed a deep sigh. "Sing me to sleep," she whispered, her voice like dry wind sweeping over the wild pampas grass.

Gently I pushed the hammock to and fro. And then, softly, I sang the lullaby she had taught me, that day when we first played with our village by the ancient stone beam, with the rain drumming on the palm fronds above us, the same lullaby her mother had sung to her:

"When the rain is falling,
When the rice is growing,
When the day is done,
Then my little one, my lovely one,
Will come home to sleep—and dream."

I watched Baby's eyes flutter as he fought sleep for a few minutes, before they closed, heavy-lidded. His breathing became deep and regular.

Jantu, too, watched over him until he was asleep. Yet even after that, she did not close her own eyes. Glowing with a dull sheen, they gazed through me, at something far away. She had a strangely remote smile on her face.

I kept rocking the hammock, and singing, and eventually Jantu closed her eyes, too, and it seemed as if she was closing herself off from me, and my song, and the world around us. And it was then that the fear and the dread welled up in me again. I wanted to shake her, to wake her up so she would come back to me.

But I only kept singing. Even after Jantu's long, slim fingers went limp, I kept on singing. I rocked and I sang, and I sang and I rocked, not daring to stop, for fear of waking the baby, but more than that, deeper than that, for fear of finding out that my friend Jantu would never wake up again.

Chapter 17

I was still rocking the hammock when the others came back. Sarun was walking slightly ahead of Nea and Mother and seemed to be in a state of high excitement. He was saying loudly over his shoulder to them, "I don't care what the rest of you think! I'm going to enlist! I've made up my mind. It is the only patriotic thing to do."

"Not so loud," I warned Sarun. "You'll wake them up." Jantu and her baby brother lay quietly curled together in the hammock. It seemed terribly important that they not be disturbed yet. I tugged at the hammock rope, careful to keep it swinging with the same gentle rhythm.

Sarun ignored me. "Did you see the way hundreds of men enlisted after the speech?" he asked the others, his voice as strident as before.

"Be quiet," I begged him. "You'll wake them up!"

Sarun glanced at the hammock. "So let them wake up!" he said loudly. "Let them see what a real soldier looks like!" He grabbed the rope from me and gave it a wild tug.

"No!" I cried, trying to snatch the rope back from him.

"Time to wake up!" Sarun announced.

I pulled the rope back from him, desperately trying to steady the hammock.

But it was too late.

The baby woke up, wailing.

I let go of the rope and watched it trail across the dust, following the hammock. Wake up, Jantu, I begged silently, please wake up.

The hammock slowed down, little by little, until it stopped swinging and reached a complete stop.

The baby kept wailing, but Jantu—Jantu did not wake up.

As if in a dream, I watched Nea pick up the baby and comfort him. Then she bent over the hammock and reached out to touch Jantu's cheek. I watched as a slow understanding dawned on Nea's face. She uttered a small cry. I watched as Mother and Grandpa Kem rushed to the hammock and looked inside. I felt numb, and though I was standing right there, I felt that I was very far away, as if I were watching it all from a great distance.

Nea was crying now, her head buried in the baby's neck as he sobbed, too. Sarun patted her back awkwardly, trying to comfort her.

"She's gone," Nea was sobbing. "She's gone, and I want to go, too. I want to go home. I want to go home." Like a kite string suddenly snapped in two and left to flail in the wind before dropping down, Nea went limp and helpless. Mother and Grandpa Kem stood quietly nearby, too stunned to do anything.

"Nea's right," I said. "It's time to go home."

"We can't leave right now," Sarun said.

"Why not?" I asked.

"Because I've decided to enlist as a regular in the army, that's why. I belong here now. I'm not going to leave."

I felt a chill go through me. "Enlist?" I said softly. "You don't mean it."

Sarun looked at me. "I do," he said.

"Why?"

"You wouldn't understand," he said. "It has to do with being a soldier. With defending the revolutionary cause. It has to do with a man's courage."

It scared me, how much I hated my brother then.

I took a deep breath. "Courage?" I echoed. "You talk of courage? What courage does it take to shoot a girl walking home in the dark? What courage did it take to kill Jantu?" My voice broke, and I wanted to crumple up and cry, too, the way Nea was doing. But Jantu had told me to be strong. Jantu had said I had to believe in myself.

I looked into the hammock at her and saw the lump of clay still cupped in her hand. You have to do it yourself, she had said; you have to make your own magic marble. I bent over and picked up the clay. It was damp and cool and heavy. Hesitantly I started to roll it between my hands. And as I rolled it, I began to feel calmer.

"What about going home?" I said, my voice controlled now. "What about planting rice and raising a family? What about trying to live in peace, when there is a war going on? Doesn't that take courage, too?"

Sarun avoided my eyes. "You're just a child, Dara," he said. "You wouldn't understand war."

"Don't tell me I don't understand war," I said fiercely. My hands seemed to have a life of their own, kneading and rolling, shaping that cool ball of clay. "I understand that Jantu will never wake up in that hammock again. I understand that Father will never come home to us again. I understand that war kills people who aren't even fighting in it." My eyes stung, and when I blinked, I could feel the threads of cool tears streaking my cheeks. But my hands were still shaping my marble, smoothing it, and I did not bother to wipe my tears away. "What I don't understand, Sarun, is why you want to fight. You said you'd take us home. The carts are all packed. The caravan is waiting. Why can't we go, Sarun? Why can't you stop fighting, and take us home?"

For a moment my brother looked up at me, and his eyes were bewildered and lost, too. Then he shook his head. "Because I am going to enlist," he said. "And as a soldier I have to stay on to fight this war. As for going home to plant rice—any woman or child can do that."

The ball of clay grew smoother and rounder. "You're right, Sarun," I said quietly. "Anyone can do that. So that's what I am going to do. I am going home now, to plant that next crop of rice."

"You?" Sarun snorted. "You and who else?"

"Just me," I answered. "I'll take a sack of our rice seed, and our oxcart, and join the caravan going to Siem Reap, and once I'm back home, I will find people to help plant the seeds with me. I'll fix up our house, repair the floorboards and the thatching on the roof. I'll tend the rice fields, and feel the raindrops on my skin, and listen to the cry of crickets at night. I've had enough of this horrible place, Sarun. I'm leaving." My voice and my hands were trembling, but the ball of clay was very smooth now.

For a long moment no one said anything. Then my mother stepped forward and stood beside me. "I'm coming with you, Dara," she said gently. "I don't think I can bear to be here much longer either. And without Jantu, there is no reason to delay our trip anymore."

Sarun's mouth dropped. "You . . . you can't do that," he said.

Mother looked at him. "Why not?" she asked.

Sarun turned to Nea. "Talk some sense into them, will you?" he demanded. "They can't take the cart and leave, just like that. It's ridiculous."

Nea shifted the baby over to her other hip. In the twilight, her tears still shone wet on her cheeks. "It's not ridiculous," she said. "It's the only sensible thing to do. And I'm going with them. And bringing Baby with me, too."

She looked at Grandpa Kem. "Are you coming?" she asked.

Grandpa Kem nodded. Then, without a word, he walked over to his oxcart. "It's all ready to go," he said. "And I'm ready to go with it."

We all watched Sarun. He looked hard at each of us, then at the oxcarts. He turned to me, his eyes angry and dazed. "I thought I was the head of the family," he said shakily. "You can't make decisions like that."

"You are still the head of our family," I said quietly. The marble was big and heavy in my hand. I kept molding it, my movements deft and sure now. "We need you to come home with us, brother. Please come."

Sarun stared at me, almost as if I were a stranger to him. For a moment I thought he was going to turn away, but he was only laying down his gun. With his bare hands outstretched, he walked slowly toward Nea.

"All right," he told her quietly. "The monsoon rains are coming soon. It's time to go home and plow the fields."

Wordlessly, Nea took his hands in hers.

It was then that I was aware of my own hands, still clenched tightly together. I relaxed, and opened up my hands. In the dappled play of light and shadow from the web of sunlit leaves above, it was hard to make out at first what I was holding. Only gradually could I see that cupped in my palm was a perfectly smooth, perfectly round marble.

I looked away at Jantu's cupped hand, now empty and lying motionless in the hammock. I did it, Jantu, I told her silently. I made my own magic marble.

Chapter 18

It was still dark when I woke up. Turning toward the opening of the thatched shelter, I looked out at the night sky. A full moon gleamed through a web of branches, and a bright morning star shone near it. The only hint of dawn was a faint glow to the east, so dim it was just a pale shade of gold-gray.

Why had I woken up so early? There had been no sudden noise, no clap of thunder, no gunfire or sound of shelling. Except for the whine of a mosquito, it was absolutely quiet. What had woken me up? And why did the morning feel so special?

Then I remembered: today was the day we were to leave.

Even now I could hardly believe it. Was it really happening, what I had dreamed of for so long? Yes, I reassured myself, we were going home, all of us, my family and Jantu's.

Jantu. That familiar heaviness, like an ache deep inside, settled on me again. The day after she died, we had taken her to the small clearing deep in the forest where two low brick walls had been built for cremations. I had gathered some wildflowers from the woods that morning and placed a bouquet of wild cleome and morning glories over her. The flowers had already wilted, and I did not stay to see them crinkle up in the flames.

Thinking about Jantu now, I wished I had given her something more, something that I had woven or shaped, something I had made, like all the things she had made and given me.

I sat up and took my two magic marbles out of my

shirt pocket. The larger one was Jantu's, and the smaller one mine. I could have given her these two marbles, I thought. But what use would she have had for them? I looked at the marbles now, and the ache inside me grew sharper. I miss you, I told Jantu; I wish you were coming with us.

Nearby, the others were beginning to stir. My mother had already rolled up her sleeping mat and slipped outside. Through the cracks in the loose thatching, I could see her gathering an armful of straw to feed the oxen. Nea was up, too, stoking the embers of the cooking fire to warm up some cold rice for a quick breakfast.

"Dara," Nea was calling. "Come have some rice now. We'll be leaving right after we eat."

I took a deep breath and slipped the two marbles back into my pocket. Then I went outside.

There was a general sense of excitement in the air. My brother had begun to hitch up the carts, and Grandpa Kem was helping him. Mother was folding the last of the sarongs she had washed and hung out the night before. Even Baby was busy, crawling around and exploring the ground under the oxcarts.

I saw a lone figure slip out of the shadows of the nearby trees and hurry toward us. Even before I could see his face, I knew it was Chnay. I was surprised, but glad, too. Ever since I had found my own family, he had avoided me, even though I had invited him to eat with us several times. But he had always refused, claiming that he felt more comfortable eating by himself. I waved to him now, and waited for him to come up to me.

"I . . . I brought you something," he said awkwardly. He held out a wooden cowbell, polished to such a high sheen that it gleamed in the morning light.

"Where did you get it?" I asked.

Chnay smiled. "I made it," he said with pride.

I thought of the way he used to break Jantu's toys, smashing them to the ground and laughing. It was hard to think of him making anything.

He must have seen the surprise on my face, because he smiled. "The first two bells I carved didn't turn out very well. This is my third try."

"Thanks, Chnay," I said.

"Actually," Chnay said, awkwardly, "I made it for Jantu. At least, I was thinking about her when I made it." He walked over to our pair of oxen and started to tie the bell around the bigger one's neck. I went over to the ox and stood on its other side. As he busied himself with tying the bell, Chnay continued, "I thought of the way she used to make things out of sticks and scraps and mud and, well . . . I felt bad that I had broken so many of them."

"Jantu would have liked your bell very much," I said shyly, stroking the muzzle of the ox. It tossed its head, swinging its new bell. It was a lovely sound, the low wooden knock-knock of it. Chnay and I smiled at each other.

"Why don't you come back with us?" I said. "You'll like our village."

He kept smiling, but his eyes turned sad. "I wouldn't belong there," he said.

"You think you belong here?"

Chnay shrugged. "Here, at least I won't feel so out of place. I mean, there are a lot of loners like me, boys without any family." Chnay paused. "I've gotten to know some of them already. And guess what? I've made friends with that monkey, too." He flashed me a smile, and then he was gone, running off without a backward glance, his bare feet kicking up sprays of water as he splashed through the puddles between the trees.

By midmorning everything was ready. Our oxen were hitched to the two oxcarts, each bulging with its pile of rice bags and tools, and the blue tarp stretched on top. Nearby, in a crooked line, the other oxcarts in the caravan were waiting, ready to start.

"Climb up," Sarun shouted over to me.

I walked over to our oxcart and climbed onto the wooden plank in front. There I took a last look around.

On the parade ground, soldiers were still doing their drills, and beyond them, I could hear the rhythmic pounding of rice seed in the little shed. Behind the grove of jacaranda trees, over the thatched roof of the kitchen, I could see the blue-and-white Khmer Serei flag, fluttering in the morning breeze.

Nea climbed up, too, and sat next to me, hugging the baby to her.

In the cart in front of us sat Grandpa Kem and my mother, looking radiant. Sarun was going to walk alongside their cart, leading the oxen.

As if sensing the excitement, the animals were pawing at the ground and tossing their heads up and down. People ran about, calling out farewells, gathering a few stray belongings, making last-minute checks of the harnesses or the ropes, before climbing onto their oxcarts.

Then the team leader stood straight up in the first cart and flicked his whip high in the air. "Hooo!" he shouted, and his oxen lumbered forward, pulling the cart along with them.

Mother's cart was the next. Sarun turned around, his eyes shining. "Ready?" he called and, without waiting for our answer, tugged the oxen forward.

It was our turn now.

"You take the reins," Nea said excitedly. "I've got Baby." I gripped the reins in my hand so tightly that my fingers felt numb.

"Come on," Nea urged me.

I nodded, then tugged at the reins. Creaking loudly, the wheels started rolling. Behind me, I could hear driver after driver shouting at his oxen, as each started up his cart in turn.

Farther ahead, Sarun was guiding his oxen on a path into the forest, away from the camp's clearing. The path that wound through the trees was narrow and uneven, edged with long puddles where previous ruts had filled with rainwater.

Following Sarun's oxcart, I pulled at my reins, veering the oxen onto the narrow path. There was a big bump as a cartwheel dipped into a rut.

As we lurched forward, the bigger of the two clay marbles inside my pocket flew out into the air and rolled into a puddle.

"Jantu's marble!" I cried. I tried to rein in the oxen, but they just plodded along, intent on following the cart ahead. Frantically I stood up, prepared to jump off the cart after the marble.

"What're you doing?" Nea asked, alarmed.

"Jantu's marble! It slipped out and—"

"We can't stop for it. You'll hold up the whole caravan!"

"But she made it! It's all I have of her." I was on the verge of tears. "It's her magic marble."

Nea reached out and put her hand on my shoulder. "The magic was never in the marble, sister," she said. "It was in Jantu. And now it's in you."

For a long moment I stared at the puddle into which Jantu's marble had disappeared. The last ripple had faded, and there was not a trace of the clay marble left. Slowly I took the other marble out of my pocket, the one I had made myself, and held it. Round and smooth and hard, it lay there in my palm.

I looked at it, and for the first time I saw it for what it was: just a lump of clay. There was no magic in it, I realized. Not in the one Jantu made, nor in the one I made. And then I finally understood what Jantu had meant when she had said the magic is in the making of the marble.

I held my marble a moment longer. Then I stood up in the oxcart and, taking a deep breath, flung the marble away.

It sailed through the air, rolled to the side of the road, and slipped into the same strip of puddle as Jantu's marble. There was a tiny splash, a few ripples, and then it, too, was gone.

I sat back down and snapped the reins. The oxen lumbered forward, and the cartwheels turned a little faster. Our cart rolled ahead, smooth and fast.

Nearby a skylark sang, perched on a sandalwood tree. The morning air was fresh and cool, and the sky a cloudless blue. Through the trees in the forest, I could see patches of vibrant green rice seedlings, rippling in the breeze.

And all around me was the sound of cowbells, the brass ones tinkling, the bamboo ones tapping like tiny drums, the shiny bronze ones jangling; but the most beautiful sound of them all was the low knocking of the wooden bell dangling from our own ox.

I tossed my head back and laughed out loud, in sheer joy. I'm going home, I thought, and I don't need magic marbles anymore. After all, the magic isn't in the marble. It's in me!

Afterword

That was over ten years ago.

We have been lucky, my family and I. We were among those to return from the Border safely and settle back into our village in Siem Reap. We planted our first crop with the precious rice seed we were given at Nong Chan, and our harvest that year was a good one.

Sarun and Nea have three children now, two boys and a girl. They live just across the fields from us. Mother lives with them, but comes to visit me almost every other day.

The years have been difficult, but we have survived. Cambodia is still a country at war, and there continues to be fighting in scattered areas, especially around the Border, but so far it has not touched us directly. There are still heavily armed soldiers there, the Khmer Rouge and Khmer Serei and the Khmer People's National Liberation Front, still merging and splitting into uneasy alliances with one another and against the Vietnamese-backed Heng Samrin government. Sometimes over the radio I hear reports of a peace plan being negotiated in some foreign city, but nothing ever seems to come of it. Meanwhile, the war continues, and the fighting continues. It makes no more sense to me now than when I was a little girl at the Border.

I don't think about what happened on the Border very much anymore. But sometimes, on an afternoon like this, when the monsoon wind is stirring the palm fronds, when the skies are alive with swallows and homemade kites, diving and dipping above the green paddy fields, when the young rice stalks ripple in sweeping waves, then I sit on the steps of our little house, and the images of the Border sweep like swallows through my mind.

I see many sad things—that gaunt hollow-eyed boy with no legs, reaching for his water bottle; those silent women, pounding the rice seed into bits of broken grain; the lost little girl with the broken doll, crying for her mother.

But of Jantu I have only happy images. I see her the way she was at the well the first day, bossy, cheerful, loud. I see her running after the food truck, hitching Baby up her hip as she ran. I see her singing her lullaby in the twilight after the rain, her eyes shining, to our little clay dolls.

I make pretty good clay dolls myself now. I shape farmers and plump babies, buffaloes and ducks, and give them to my daughter to play with. That's right, I have a daughter now, a toddler with chubby fingers and sparkling eyes. My husband dotes on her and is always urging me to make her more clay toys.

There is one thing I haven't made for her, and that is a clay marble. I know I can make them, the way Jantu taught me, smooth and round and hard. But I am not going to make any yet. When the time comes, I want to teach her how to make a magic marble, for herself.

Related Readings

CONTENTS

All the People of Khmer Were Very Troubled

by Ven Yem

What was life like for Cambodians under the Khmer Rouge regime and during the Vietnamese occupation? This autobiographical account, recorded at the Philippine Refugee Processing Center by Joanna C. Scott, is taken from Scott's book Indochina's Refugees: Oral Histories from Laos, Cambodia, and Vietnam.

My name is Ven Yem. I am Khmer. I want to tell about what happened in my country and why I decided to leave.

Pol Pot's regime occupied Cambodia in 1975 and all the people of Khmer were very troubled. The towns and the cities were full of Pol Pot's soldiers and they displaced all the people from the cities and the towns to live in the countryside. They divided them into three groups, men, women and children, and set them to build big canals and to work in the rice fields.

I had been a farmer and a goldsmith. I had my own farm, about 30 *rite* (one *rite* is 1,600 square meters), and I grew rice. Pol Pot's Communists took away my farm. They took me away, far away from my village and from my family. I heard that my farm is now a reservoir.

For a long time then I lived with Pol Pot's regime. And I was very troubled. I had no freedom and no hope. By 1977 there was no food to support all the people. For three years the Khmer people ate only boiled rice. Into one big pan they would put just one can of rice to feed twenty or thirty people.

So they found it very hard to do the work, very hard. All the people were tired, very tired. Some died in the rice fields and some were accused of being spies and killed. I got sick because there was not food enough to eat, just boiled rice, boiled rice for a long time. I was so very tired.

We had to work very hard making a farm and digging drainage and growing food for the Communists. Sometimes we had to get up and start work very early in the morning while it was still dark—as early as three o'clock—and sometimes we had to work right through the dark night. We never got more than two or three hours' rest. There was no food in the morning until eleven o'clock, then one cup of water with some rice in it. We had the same again at five o'clock in the afternoon.

After the evening rice we had to do other work near the camp. I worked growing vegetables— cabbages, potatoes, tomatoes and also sugar cane. This food was not for us. It was for the Communists. The chairman of the village ordered it.

We lived in huts. In some huts there were thirty people, in some one hundred, in some two hundred. There were no soldiers in the huts. There was a group leader. He answered to the chairman of the village.

We could not run away. They said, "Do not try to escape. We will see you. We have many eyes, like a pineapple."

They had an action army—spies. They were chosen by the village chairman. Some were Communists who came from outside and some they recruited from amongst the people in the camp. They lived amongst us. We did not know who they were. They watched us and knew all that we did. So we were afraid.

If anyone tried to escape or if they did not work hard enough they would accuse them of being enemies of the new regime. And they would be killed. The village chairman would order it.

They kept us all together. This was so that they could have meetings with us, many meetings. There were meetings every night. They told us all we must make a new regime. We must forget the old regime. They told us we would not have monks any more. There were be no more Buddhist religion. The people were not to respect the monks. They said the monks were like leeches, sucking the blood. The Communists did not believe in religion. They wanted to do away with it and with the monks too. But the people were worried about sin.

While I was in Pol Pot's camp, my wife had been working for the Communists also. She was growing vegetables for them in our home village. There was no school for the children. They had to work in the fields too. They cut grass, piled it up and hauled it.

Then after the Pol pot occupation of my country, it was occupied a second time by Heng Semrin and the Vietnamese soldiers. They said that the soldiers of Vietnam had come to help us but I knew that Vietnam and Cambodia were not friendly. My parents and grandparents had told all the children that the soldiers of Vietnam would take the heads of Khmer people to boil their tea water. They would cut off the heads of my people and take three of them and put them on the ground in a triangle like stones. Then in the middle they would make a fire and on the heads they would support a pot of water to boil. I think these stories were true.

And so I decided, and all the Khmer people decided, to try to escape from our country because all the people in my family and my country were afraid of the troops of Vietnam. I ran away and found my wife and we made a plan to escape from my country because it was unbearable to live there. Then we ran away to the border of Khmer and Thailand.

I left my country in 1979. When I left I had five children. With my wife and myself there were seven people in my family. We came by walking and my small children I carried.

All the people were leaving my country. They did not go by the roads because the soldiers would see them. They went through the fields and through the forests.

We went from our village, from Sousey Village in Battambang Province, and walked about five days until we reached the border of Khmer and Thailand. There we met UNHCR organizers. They had a big truck and I was very happy because they took us into Thailand's country and the Khan I Dan camp.

I stayed there for a long time and had two more children. At first I worked in construction. Then I worked in food distribution to the people that lived in the camp. And after that I worked in the United Nations warehouse for three months. I was glad to do that.

After that they took me and my family and all the Khmer people to the Chunburi camp in Thailand. We stayed there two months and after two months they took us all to the airport in Bangkok and we went to Manila town. I stayed in Manila town one night and after that they took me by bus to the Philippine Refugee Processing Center camp.

I arrived in the PRPC camp August 17, 1985. I have been here about two months now. I am an assistant teacher in the evenings and in the afternoons I work in the Inter-Neighborhood Council chairman's office.

When I finish studying here I will go to the United States. I have a sister in San Francisco and I will go to San Francisco too. When I reach there my sponsor will help my family and I will find a job. I don't know yet what I will do but I must work hard to earn money for my family because now I have seven children. If I can find work as a goldsmith or on a farm I can do it. But I will do any work and I will work so hard to make America a good country for my family.

Above all, I desire and I want to drive Vietnam out of my country. I want to help my country displace the Vietnamese soldiers because all the Khmer people love their country so much but now the Vietnamese soldiers occupy all of our Cambodia. And I hope to organize all the countries in the world that love peace to help my country. [Philippine Refugee Processing Center, November 6, 1985.]

My Life Story

by Lan Nguyen

Dara's journey to find her family transforms her into a strong and determined young woman. Compare and contrast Dara's attitude toward life with that of the Vietnamese speaker of this poem.

What shall I tell about my life?

    a life of changes
    a life of losing
    remembering
5   eighteen years ago
    a little child was born
    surrounded by the love of family
    so warm and tender
    surrounded by mountains and rivers
10   so free and beautiful
    But life was not easy
    the dearest father passed away
    and left a big scar in the child's head

    She grew up with something missing in her
15   She had seen the people born and dying
        born from the war
        dying from guns and bombs

    Sometimes she wished
    she could do something
20   for herself and her people

But what could she do?

Nothing but watch and watch
for she is too small
only a sand in the big desert
25   no power
nothing at all

She is only herself
an ordinary person
carrying a dream
30   that seems so far, far, far away

The only thing she can do
is keep hoping
one day her dream will come true

God cannot be mean to her forever.

Oppression

by Langston Hughes

*Just as Pol Pot and the Khmer Rouge
tyrannized the people of Cambodia, other
forces have oppressed, or kept down, the
people of other nations, societies, and
races. What happens to the dreams of
those who are persecuted?*

Now dreams
Are not available
To the dreamers,
Nor songs
5 To the singers.

In some lands
Dark night
And cold steel
Prevail—
10 But the dream
Will come back,
And the song
Break
Its jail.

Birthday Box

by Jane Yolen

*Jantu's gift of the clay marble helps Dara
feel the confidence she needs to journey
on alone. It changes Dara in ways she
never imagined. Who knows how a gift
might influence a person's future?*

I was ten years old when my mother died. Ten
years old on that very day. Still she gave me a party
of sorts. Sick as she was, Mama had seen to it,
organizing it at the hospital. She made sure the
doctors and nurses all brought me presents. We were
good friends with them all by that time, because
Mama had been in the hospital for so long.

The head nurse, V. Louise Higgins (I never did
know what that *V* stood for), gave me a little box,
which was sort of funny because she was the biggest
of all the nurses there. I mean she was tremendous.
And she was the only one who insisted on wearing
all white. Mama had called her the great white shark
when she was first admitted, only not to V. Louise's
face. "All those needles," Mama had said. "Like
teeth." But V. Louise was sweet, not sharklike at all,
and she'd been so gentle with Mama.

I opened the little present first. It was a fountain
pen, a real one, not a fake one like you get at Kmart.

"Now you can write beautiful stories, Katie," V.
Louise said to me.

I didn't say that stories come out of your head, not
out of a pen. That wouldn't have been polite, and
Mama—even sick—was real big on politeness.

"Thanks, V. Louise," I said.

The Stardust Twins—which is what Mama called Patty and Tracey-lynn because they reminded her of dancers in an old-fashioned ballroom—gave me a present together. It was a diary and had a picture of a little girl in pink, reading in a garden swing. A little young for me, a little too cute. I mean, I read Stephen King and want to write like him. But as Mama always reminded me whenever Dad finally remembered to send me something, it was the thought that counted, not the actual gift.

"It's great," I told them. "I'll write in it with my new pen." And I wrote my name on the first page just to show them I meant it.

They hugged me and winked at Mama. She tried to wink back but was just too tired and shut both her eyes instead

Lily, who is from Jamaica, had baked me some sweet bread. Mary Margaret gave me a gold cross blessed by the pope, which I put on even though Mama and I weren't churchgoers. That was Dad's thing.

Then Dr. Dann, the intern who was on days, and Dr. Pucci, the oncologist (which is the fancy name for a cancer doctor), gave me a big box filled to the top with little presents, each wrapped up individually. All things they knew I'd love—paperback books and writing paper and erasers with funny animal heads and colored paper clips and a rubber stamp that printed FROM KATIE'S DESK and other stuff. They must have raided a stationery store.

There was one box, though, they held out till the end. It was about the size of a large top hat. The paper was deep blue and covered with stars; not fake stars but real stars, I mean, like a map of the night sky. The ribbon was two shades of blue with silver threads running through. There was no name on the card.

"Who's it from?" I asked.

None of the nurses answered, and the doctors both suddenly were studying the ceiling tiles with the kind of intensity they usually saved for X rays. No one spoke. In fact the only sound for the longest time was Mama's breathing machine going in and out and in and out. It was a harsh, horrible, insistent sound, and usually I talked and talked to cover up the noise. But I was waiting for someone to tell me.

At last V. Louise said, "It's from your mama, Katie. She told us what she wanted. And where to get it."

I turned and looked at Mama then, and her eyes were open again. Funny, but sickness had made her even more beautiful than good health had. Her skin was like that old paper, the kind they used to write on with quill pens, and stretched out over her bones so she looked like a model. Her eyes, which had been a deep, brilliant blue, were now like the fall sky, bleached and softened. She was like a faded photograph of herself. She smiled a very small smile at me. I knew it was an effort.

"It's you," she mouthed. I read her lips. I had gotten real good at that. I thought she meant it was a present for me.

"Of course it is," I said cheerfully. I had gotten good at that, too, being cheerful when I didn't feel like it. "Of course it is."

I took the paper off the box carefully, not tearing it but folding it into a tidy packet. I twisted the ribbons around my hand and then put them on the pillow by her hand. It made the stark white hospital bed look almost festive.

Under the wrapping, the box was beautiful itself. It was made of a heavy cardboard and covered with a linen material that had a pattern of cloudfilled skies.

I opened the box slowly and . . .

"It's empty," I said. "Is this a joke?" I turned to ask Mama, but she was gone. I mean, her body was there, but she wasn't. It was as if she was as empty as the box.

Dr. Pucci leaned over her and listened with a stethoscope, then almost absently patted Mama's head. Then, with infinite care, V. Louise closed Mama's eyes, ran her hand across Mama's cheek, and turned off the breathing machine.

"Mama!" I cried. And to the nurses and doctors, I screamed, "Do something!" And because the room had suddenly become so silent, my voice echoed back at me. "Mama, do something."

. . .

I cried steadily for, I think, a week. Then I cried at night for a couple of months. And then for about a year I cried at anniversaries, like Mama's birthday or mine, at Thanksgiving, on Mother's Day. I stopped writing. I stopped reading except for school assignments. I was pretty mean to my half brothers and totally rotten to my stepmother and Dad. I felt empty and angry, and they all left me pretty much alone.

And then one night, right after my first birthday without Mama, I woke up remembering how she had said, "It's you." Not, "It's for you," just "It's you." Now Mama had been a high school English teacher and a writer herself. She'd had poems published in little magazines. She didn't use words carelessly. In the end she could hardly use any words at all. So—I asked myself in that dark room—why had she said,

"It's you"? Why were they the very last words she had ever said to me, forced out with her last breath?

I turned on the bedside light and got out of bed. The room was full of shadows, not all of them real.

Pulling the desk chair over to my closet, I climbed up and felt along the top shelf, and against the back wall, there was the birthday box, just where I had thrown it the day I had moved in with my dad.

I pulled it down and opened. it. It was as empty as the day I had put it away.

"It's you," I whispered to the box.

And then suddenly I knew.

Mama had meant *I* was the box, solid and sturdy, maybe even beautiful or at least interesting on the outside. But I had to fill up the box to make it all it could be. And I had to fill me up as well. She had guessed what might happen to me, had told me in a subtle way. In the two words she could manage.

I stopped crying and got some paper out of the desk drawer. I got out my fountain pen. I started writing, and I haven't stopped since. The first thing I wrote was about that birthday. I put it in the box, and pretty soon that box was overflowing with stories. And poems. And memories.

And so was I.

And so was I.

Holes

by Lillian Morrison

Like many victims of war, Dara is forced to cope
with the death of many people who are important
to her. How might Dara respond to this speaker's
views on the death of a loved one?

Strangest of gaps
their goneness—
mother, father, loved friends

the black holes
5   of the astronomer
are not more mysterious

this kind of hole
will not be filled
with candle flames
10   or even a thousand thoughts

the hole is inside us
it brims over
is empty and full at once.

from Childhood and Poetry

by Pablo Neruda
translated by Robert Bly

Nea, Jantu, and Chnay all offered gifts in the spirit of friendship. In this selection, the Chilean poet and diplomat Pablo Neruda reflects on his beliefs about the importance of reaching out to others.

One time, investigating in the backyard of our house in Temuco the tiny objects and minuscule beings of my world, I came upon a hole in one of the boards of the fence. I looked through the hole and saw a landscape like that behind our house, uncared for, and wild. I moved back a few steps, because I sensed vaguely that something was about to happen. All of a sudden a hand appeared—a tiny hand of a boy about my own age. By the time I came close again, the hand was gone, and in its place there was a marvelous white sheep.

The sheep's wool was faded. Its wheels had escaped. All of this only made it more authentic. I had never seen such a wonderful sheep. I looked back through the hole but the boy had disappeared. I went into the house and brought out a treasure of my own: a pinecone, opened, full of odor and resin, which I adored. I set it down in the same spot and went off with the sheep.

I never saw either the hand or the boy again. And I have never again seen a sheep like that either. The toy I lost finally in a fire. But even now, in 1954, almost fifty years old, whenever I pass a toy shop, I look furtively into the window, but it's no use. They don't make sheep like that anymore.

I have been a lucky man. To feel the intimacy of brothers is a marvelous thing in life. To feel the love of people whom we love is a fire that feeds our life. But to feel the affection that comes from those whom we do not know, from those unknown to use, who are watching over our sleep and solitude, over our dangers and our weaknesses—that is something still greater and more beautiful because it widens out the boundaries of our being, and unites all living things.

That exchange brought home to me for the first time a precious idea: that all of humanity is somehow together. That experience came to me again much later; this time it stood out strikingly against a background of trouble and persecution.

It won't surprise you then that I attempted to give something resiny, earthlike, and fragrant in exchange for human brotherhood. Just as I once left the pinecone by the fence, I have since left my words on the door of so many people who were unknown to me, people in prison, or hunted, or alone.

That is the great lesson I learned in my childhood, in the backyard of a lonely house. Maybe it was nothing but a game two boys played who didn't know each other and wanted to pass to the other some good things of life. Yet maybe this small and mysterious exchange of gifts remained inside me also, deep and indestructible, giving my poetry light.

All-Ball

by Mary Pope Osborne

*At first, Dara thinks the clay marble is the
source of the strength of character she
displays. The narrator in this account
needs strength of a different kind. Where
does a person get the strength to survive
difficulties, such as hardship and loss?*

I remember the first time I got really bad news.

I was eight years old, and my family was living in
white wooden army quarters at the edge of a thick
pine forest in Fort Eustis, Virginia. All my life we had
lived on military posts, and I loved them. I loved the
neat lawns, clean streets, trim houses, and starched
uniforms. I loved parade bands, marching troops,
green jeeps, tanks, and transport trucks. I loved
having military police at the entrance gate. When I
was four, I dreamed that the M.P.'s guarding the gate
chased away a couple of ghosts that tried to come
onto our post. It is one of the most vivid dreams I've
ever had, and to this day, it makes me feel good to
remember it.

Living on an army post in those days was so safe
that in all the early summers of our lives the children
of our family were let out each morning like
dandelions to the wind. My teenage sister went off
with her friends while my brothers and I filled our
time playing with out toy soldiers, including my
favorite—a small silver statue of General Omar
Bradley. We played "maneuvers" by carrying large
cardboard boxes around the parade field, stopping

every hundred yards to "bivouac" by making grass beds and napping inside our boxes.

At five o'clock, when the bugle played and the flag was lowered, we went home. Our return was often punctuated by the joyous sight of our dad stepping out of a chauffeured military car, his arms raised to embrace us.

But one spring night when I was eight, bad news changed everything. I remember my dad was helping me prepare my bath. I was sitting on the edge of the tub while the water ran, and Dad was standing in the doorway, wearing his summer khaki uniform. "Sis—" he always called me Sis or Little Bits—"in six weeks, Daddy is going to Korea."

I looked at him and burst into tears. I knew we wouldn't be going with him. Though the Korean War had ended eight years earlier, U.S. soldiers were still sent there for tours of duty—without their families.

"Don't cry," he said. "I'll only be gone for a year."

Only a year?

"While I'm gone, you'll live in Florida, in Daytona Beach, near the ocean."

Daytona Beach? Away from an army post?

"You'll have a wonderful time."

"No I won't!" I hated this news. And to prove it, I pushed him out of the bathroom.

Of course, I was right and he was wrong. A few weeks later, when Dad drove our family to Daytona Beach to get us settled, I didn't find our new life wonderful at all.

Our house was low to the ground, flamingo-pink, and made of stucco. There were no kids in the whole neighborhood. There were no real trees in our small yard—just a few scrubby ones. There was no wide open parade field to play on.

I recoiled from this new life—especially when I

discovered lizards scampering across our cement driveway, a huge water bug scuttling across the floor of the TV room, and a gigantic black spider hovering in the corner of the garage. Such monsters didn't exist on army posts—neither did the crazy variety of houses, the litter, the tawdry seaside billboards.

Adding to the trauma of adjusting to life off a military post was the awareness that my dad was leaving in just three weeks. At first, I tried to manage my grief by taking a little time out of every day to cry. In those days, I was very organized. I kept a daily list of things to do like:

Wash hands
Play with dolls
Practice writing
Practice running

I added "Cry for Daddy" to the list. But as I counted down the days till his departure, I began to cry even when it wasn't schedule. Worse, I abandoned the other things on my list to keep a watch on my dad. I studied everything he did—from buying a vanilla ice-cream cone at the Dairy Queen to playing catch with my brothers—because I felt I had to store up enough memories of him to last through the coming year.

The pressure became unbearable and soon forced me into the strangest relationship of my life. Just thinking about this relationship now can bring tears to my eyes. Was it with a wonderful girl? Boy? Grown-up? Dog, cat, parakeet?

No. It was with a *ball*.

About two weeks before Dad left, he took my brothers and me to a Rose's Five & Dime store. He gave us fifty cents each to buy whatever we wanted.

This is the most precious fifty cents I will ever spend, I thought. Slowly, I wandered the rows of comics, coloring books, plastic dolls, and bags of candy, looking for an object worthy of the last-fifty-cents-my-father-gave-me-before-he-went-to-Korea.

When I came to the ball section, I saw, amidst a variety of balls, a truly unique specimen: a nubby rubber ball, bigger than a softball and smaller than a kickball. It was made up of swirling pastel colors— pink, blue, green.

I picked up the ball and bounced it.

It was the best bouncing ball I'd ever encountered. Barely did it touch the wooden floor before it sprang back into my hands. The ball felt friendly, spunky, and vibrant. It had such a positive and strong personality that I named it before we even got home: All-Ball.

For the next twelve days. All-Ball and I were inseparable. I bounced him on the driveway and on the sidewalk. Standing apart from everyone, deep in my own world, I bounced him for hours. And while I bounced, I talked to myself. I invented stories. Not dramatic stories of high-adventure. But stories about ordinary families—families in which everyone stayed together and everyone was safe and secure.

In these families, there was perfect order. The children all had names that began with the same letter—David, Danny, and Doris; Paul, Peter, and Patsy; Anne, Alice, Adam, and Ace.

I gave the children ages, personalities, and dialogue. I played all the parts. I was John joking with Jane; Jane laughing with Jack; Adam telling a story to Ace; Alice describing her school outfits to Anne.

I lived in different families morning, afternoon, and twilight. I could only create these worlds with All-Ball's help. His sprightly, joyous attitude gave me confidence. The sound of his rhythmic bounce banished my fears. His constant presence eased the sorrow of Dad's leaving. In fact, whenever Dad tried to engage me in conversation or play, I turned away from him. I stopped paying attention to him altogether.

I had fallen in love with a ball.

Though everyone in my family must have thought my behavior odd, they adjusted quickly. Within a day or two, they were treating "Sis's ball" sort of like a family pet.

No one, however, was fully aware of the depth of my attachment until the morning All-Ball was destroyed.

It was a hot, bright July morning—just two days before Dad was to leave for Korea. I was outside before everyone else, bouncing All-Ball on the sidewalk, inventing a family with a neat number of years between each child. I liked the children to be ten, eight, six, four. Boy, girl, boy, girl. John, Jane, Jed, Joy.

While I was bouncing All-Ball in the early warm air, a small black dog wandered down the sidewalk to see what was up, a little dog I paid no attention to—until it was too late. And then everything happened so fast, I couldn't stop it.

I fumbled a bounce. The black dog charged and grabbed All-Ball in his mouth. He punctured the rubber skin with his teeth, then shook the deflated ball with glee, tearing it to pieces. I started to scream. I screamed and screamed.

Everyone rushed out to their yards—old people from all the quiet, lonely houses. My parents, brothers, sister. I couldn't stop screaming as I ran around, picking up all the torn patches of All-Ball. I clutched them to my chest and howled at the top of my lungs.

My mother explained to the neighbors that my ball had popped. My brothers and sister watched me in horror—my father in confusion. "We'll get you another ball," he said.

He couldn't have uttered crueler words. There was no other ball like All-Ball. Not in the whole world. Not with his spirit, his bounce, his steadfastness. I screamed "No!" with such rage that everyone retreated.

I ran inside, and, clutching the pieces of All-Ball, I went to bed, yelling at everyone to leave us alone. I kissed the pastel-colored nubby skin and sobbed and sobbed.

I did not get up all day. I grieved for the death of All-Ball with all the grief my eight years could muster. I was brought lunch, cool drinks, newspaper comics, wet washcloths for my head, children's aspirin. But nothing worked. I would not get up. I would not let go of the torn pieces of the ball.

At twilight, I could hear the family having dinner in the dining room. My mother had the decency to allow me to work out my sorrow on my own. I don't think she even allowed anyone to laugh.

As light faded across my room, I could hear sprinklers spritzing outside, and an old woman calling to her cats. By now, my eyes stung and were nearly swollen shut. My throat burned. My heart had not stopped hurting all day.

"Little Bits?" My father stood in my doorway. He was holding a ball. It was mostly white with a little bit of blue.

I moaned and turned my face to the wall as he walked toward the bed.

"You won't let me give you this new ball?" he said.

"No!" I said, gasping with another wave of grief.

"Go away!"

"This ball's pretty nice," he said.

Closing my eyes, I shook my head emphatically, furious he did not understand the difference between the ball he held and All-Ball. "I hate it! Go away!"

He didn't. He sat on the edge of the bed.

But I would not look at him. My burning eyes stared at the wall. My body was stiff with anger.

"I like your barrette," he said softly.

He was referring to a pink Scottie dog barrette locked onto my tangled hair.

I didn't speak.

He cleared his throat. "I hope you'll wear that the day I come home."

I blinked. The truth was I hadn't thought much about his coming home. Only about his leaving.

"I'll bring you a ring when I come back," he said.

I didn't move. Just blinked again.

"What kind of ring would you like?"

I mumbled something.

"What?" he asked.

"A pearl," I said hoarsely.

"A pearl ring. Okay. On the day I come home, I'll bring you a pearl ring. And a music box. How's that? I'll hide in the bushes, and when you ride up on your bike, home from school, I'll jump out and surprise you. How's that?"

He cleared his throat again. I turned just a little to look at him. I saw he had tears in his eyes. I didn't want him to feel sad too. That was almost worse than anything.

I reluctantly rolled over onto my back. I looked at the ball he held. It was still a stupid ball, no doubt about that. But I mumbled something about it being pretty.

"Will you play with this one?" he said.

I touched it with my finger. I let out a quivering sigh, then nodded, accepting the complications of the moment. All-Ball would know that he could never be replaced. Ever. He was the one and only ball for me. But I could pretend to like this other one. Even play with it. For Dad's sake.

He handed me the white ball and I embraced it and smiled feebly.

He smiled back. "Come eat some dinner with us now," he said.

I was ready. I wanted to leave my room. The light of day was nearly gone.

"Come on." He helped me off the bed, and, clutching pieces of All-Ball along with the new white ball, I joined the family.

My dad left soon after that. We entered a new school. Ball-bouncing was replaced with friends, homework, and writing letters to Korea. Still—and this is weird, I'll admit—I slept with a torn piece of All-Ball under my pillow for the next year, until after my dad came home.

Dear World, January 17, 1994

by Alma Luz Villanueva

*Peace and unrest, famine and bounty,
health and disease, wealth and poverty.
Consider the variety of conditions in which
people exist. How can a person come to
terms with the two different "worlds"
described in this poem?*

I come to the edge of
the world at 8:10 am

to see if the tide is
high or low,

5   to see if the sun is
rising in winter,

to see if ducks, wild ones,
still love the sky;

and the tide was high,
10   wild, striking cliffs

with rainbows, daily
gifts from the sun—

on the other side of
the world, people must

15   run in the streets, holding
their children's hands, hoping

the sniper will miss—
the old, the slow,

are killed, and no one
20   can touch the body

or they, too, will die—
a woman, my age, stands

on a road, her vigil, throwing
stones at trucks, full of

25   children, women like herself,
the old, screaming, YOU KILLED

MY BOY! YOU KILLED, YOU KILLED
MY BOY! Her boy, one year

younger than my son,
30   tortured, killed, made

to dig his own grave—
you see, my Earth,

I'm grateful for my life,
this magnificent world I've

come to witness—but I must
weigh her life

and mine,
daily.

Acknowledgments

(continued from page ii)

Marian Reiner, Literary Agent: "Holes," from *Overheard in a Bubble Chamber* by Lillian Morrison. Copyright © 1981 by Lillian Morrison. Reprinted by permission of Marian Reiner for the author.

Robert Bly: Excerpt from "Childhood and Poetry" by Pablo Neruda. Reprinted from *Neruda and Vallejo: Selected Poems*, edited by Robert Bly, Beacon Press, Boston, 1971, 1993. Copyright © 1971, 1993 by Robert Bly. Reprinted with the permission of Robert Bly.

Brandt & Brandt Literary Agents, Inc.: "All-Ball" by Mary Pope Osborne. Copyright © 1996 by Mary Pope Osborne. Originally appeared in *When I Was Your Age*, edited by Amy Erlich, published by Candlewick Press. Reprinted by permission of Brandt & Brandt Literary Agents, Inc.

Alma Luz Villanueva: "Dear World, January 17, 1994" by Alma Luz Villanueva. Reprinted by permission of the author.